Government Gardens

HOBART TOWN

By Mr Frankland

Commissariat Stores

The Mall

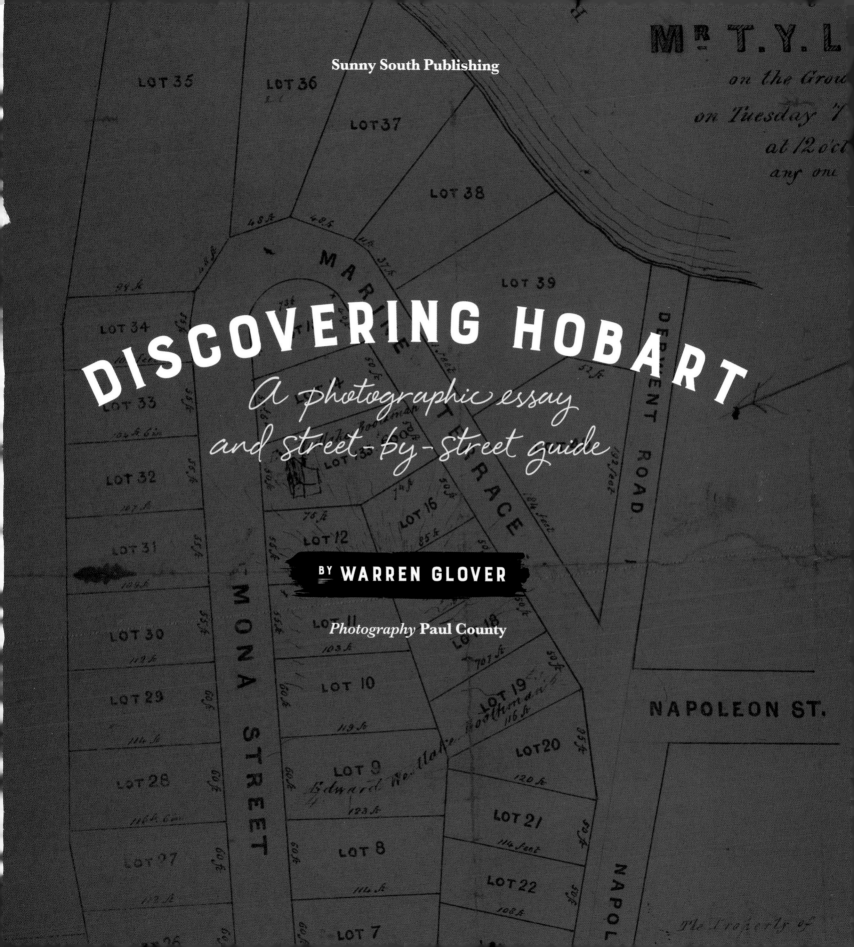

Sunny South Publishing

DISCOVERING HOBART

A photographic essay and street-by-street guide

BY WARREN GLOVER

Photography **Paul County**

Sincere thanks to

Warren Glover

Thank you to my parents who, in their own way, exposed me to the environment that is our history and then kept me inspired, thus building in me the passion for story telling and learning about the incredible human story and built heritage that unfolds during my research projects.

To my darling wife, Amy, who from the start of this project assisted me in every possible way — by granting time, emotional support, praise or constructive criticism, you made sure this book stayed on course and on time. I could not have delivered this without you and your expertise.

Thank you so very much. What a team we are, what a wonderful time spent together it has been.

Thanks to Paul County, who thankfully approached me to do this project. I could not have enjoyed it more. Working along with Paul and his great enthusiasm and passion for his work was a continual recharge for me throughout the creative process of the book. I will certainly miss our regular drive-bys and the receiving of amazing new images almost daily over the many months.

Paul County

David Newell at The Coin and Stamp Place, Hobart, Craig Jeffrey and Craig Tipping at Department of Treasury and Finance, Barry Toates at Royal Tennis Club, Barney Phillips at Citta Hobart, Trish Stagg at Hobart City Council, Nick Osborne at Osborne Images, Scott Carlin at TMAG, Phillip 'Sunny' Drury at Clemengers, Megan Turner at Wrest Point, Maria Pate and Sandy Campbell at The Theatre Royal, Kelsey Timms and Sophie Bleach at The Tench – Penitentiary Chapel Historic Site, Roseanne Warren at the GPO, David Clark at the Hobart Synagogue, Stephanie Hesford and James Reynolds at Parliament House, Kelly Luck and Claire O'Halloran at Hadleys Orient Hotel, Richard Gerathy at Premium Business, Megan Turner at Wrest Point, Matt Casey at Federal Hotels Group, Dana Clemow at The Henry Jones Art Hotel and David Owen, Official Secretary at Government House.

Discovering Hobart - a photographic essay and street-by-street guide
First published in Australia in 2016 by Sunny South Publishing, an imprint of Tas Food Books, Taroona Tasmania
www.tasfoodbooks.com

Copyright on behalf of all copyright holders © Tas Food Books 2016

Image credits: Rosie Hastie, courtesy of City of Hobart pages 75, 76 (Town Hall interiors), Andy Wilson page 162 (Lenna interiors), MONA image courtesy Mona Museum, Chris Bennett (St Mary's Hospital) page 98, Nick Osborne page 94 (and back cover landscape), Sam Shelley (Lark Bar) page 2, Valerie Kulrich (Beach image) page 1.

WF *four* text courtesy of Hobart City Council

Publisher   Paul Brendan County
Author   Warren Glover
Book designer   Cathy McAuliffe
Proofreader   Vicki Montgomery

Disclaimer
Although all reasonable care has been taken in the preparation of this book, neither the publisher nor the author can accept any liability for any consequence arising from the use thereof, or the information contained theirein. Any queries email the publisher info@tasfoodbooks.com.

ISBN 9780994576101

Printed and bound in China by Imago

10 9 8 7 6 5 4 3 2 1

National Library of Australia Cataloguing-in-Publication Data. A catalogue record of this book is available on request.

This book may be purchased at **www.tasfoodbooks.com**

Sunny South Publishing

DISCOVERING HOBART

A photographic essay and street-by-street guide

BY **WARREN GLOVER**

Photography **Paul County**

The Publisher wishes to acknowledge the − Mouheneenner (pronounced Moo-he-ne-nah) People, the traditional owners and custodians of the land upon which Hobart was built.

CONTENTS

HOBART CITY - STREET BY STREET

MURRAY STREET

ELIZABETH STREET

ARGYLE STREET

HARRINGTON STREET

CAMPBELL STREET

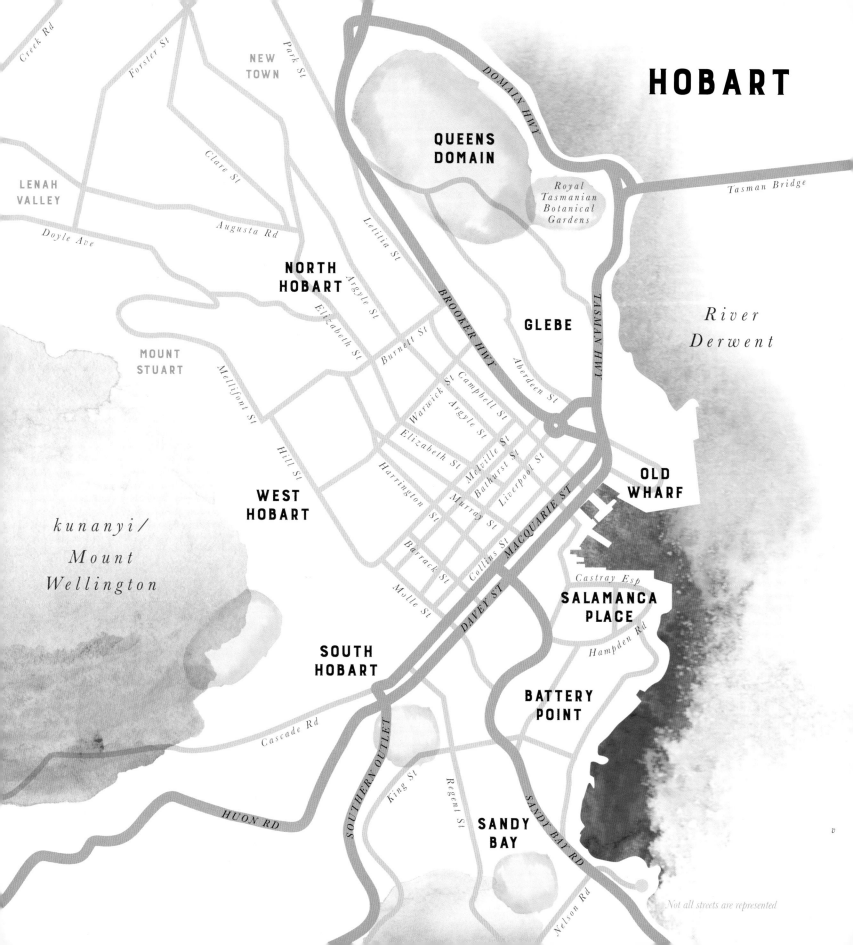

HOBART CITY - STREET BY STREET

LIVERPOOL STREET

QUEENS DOMAIN

WATERFRONT

BATTERY POINT

SANDY BAY

INTRODUCTION

There are hundreds of heritage-listed buildings in Hobart.

To keep *Discovering Hobart* manageable we selected seventy three icons.

Each icon includes some fascinating historical information by author Warren Glover and at least one image.

The book is laid out street by street so you can, if you wish, put on your walking shoes, mingle with the locals and see the buildings up close.

There are many other interesting and beautiful features along the way that you can find if you look with an observant eye, so we've included these as architectural features pages.

In the back of the book are lists of various tours you can experience and what better than to stay in heritage accommodation? This is listed, too.

We hope you'll have as much fun exploring and discovering treasures on the wonderful streets of Hobart, as we did when compiling this book.

Warren Glover and Paul County

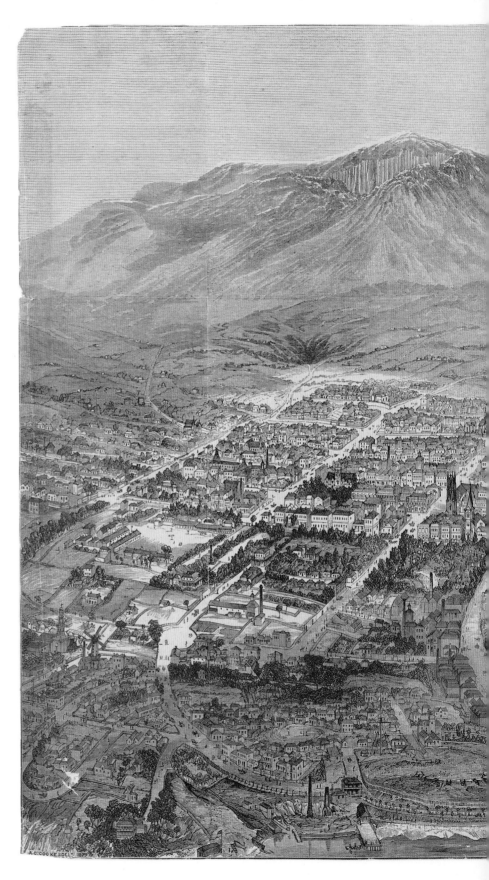

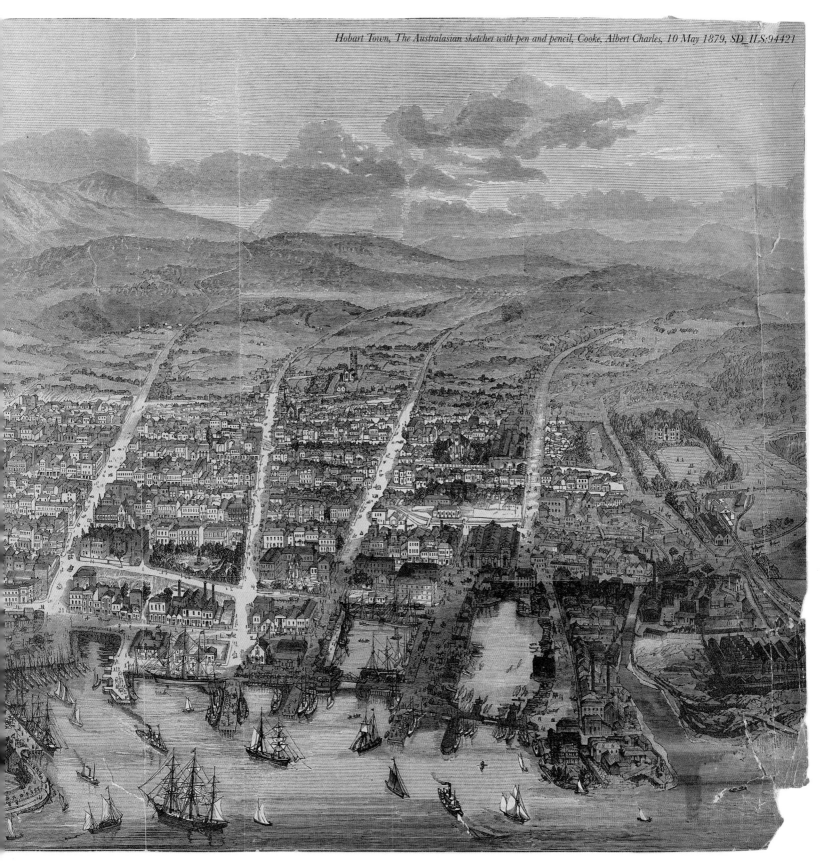

iv

About HOBART

The City of Hobart is often referred to as one of the most beautiful and livable cities in the world. In 2013 *Lonely Planet* listed it as one of the Top 10 Cities in the World to visit. As the second oldest city in Australia it offers a wonderful blend of built and cultural heritage, environment, a vibrant art scene and a low-stress lifestyle.

Within a short distance by car from the CBD, you can enjoy numerous golf courses, magnificent rural views, vineyards, distilleries and breweries, oyster farms, rain forests, long sandy beaches, surf beaches, and an exhaustive list of walks and fishing spots. Many homes in Hobart have spectacular views of the mountain, the Derwent River or the Meehan Ranges.

The southernmost capital city in Australia, Hobart is situated 42 degrees south with a cool temperate climate. During summer (December – February) average temperatures range from 11.5 - 21°C (52.7 - 69.8°F). Summer temperatures often reach into the 30s. The months of January and February are also the driest, and it's warm enough to swim at the beach. Autumn has many calm, sunny days, with average temperatures between 8.9 and 17.3°C (48 - 63.1°F). The city is blanketed in glorious red and yellow hues as the trees begin to change. During winter the island feels the southerly winds from the Antarctic and experiences some of Australia's coolest temperatures, average daily temperatures range from 5 - 12.3°C (41 - 54.1°F). During spring, average temperatures range from 7.8 - 16.9°C (46 - 62.4°F). This is the wettest time of year (168.7mm / 6.6); however, it should be noted that Hobart is Australia's second-driest capital city (after Adelaide).

St David's Park.

Snow on the beach 2015

1

In 2015 it snowed down to sea level again. Some snow-loving locals say the real problem with Hobart is that in winter it's just not cold enough!

Hobart sprawls over hills and valleys that sit below Mount Nelson and the awe-inspiring dolerite of Mount Wellington/kunanyi, which, despite Hobart's genuine four seasons, can at times see snow on its caps year-round. Snow falling in the city is very infrequent. In the 1980s, when it did, one commuter was famously snapped skiing across the Tasman Bridge to work. In 2015 it snowed down to sea level again. Some snow-loving locals say the real problem with Hobart is that in winter it's just not cold enough!

Lark Whisky Bar

Salamanca Place

Dark Mofo Winter Feast

Salamanca Place is a must-see for visitors to Hobart; old sandstone warehouses host galleries and many quality eateries. Nearby is Battery Point, a quaint historic district with narrow lanes and colonial-era cottages.

Hobart's rich colonial architecture and natural charms are complemented by an all-year-round series of art and music festivals and markets and award-winning hotels and restaurants providing mostly excellent local produce, its journey often from the farm gate to the table.

Tourism is one of Hobart's major industries. Appreciation for such a boutique city is at its height, as larger cities often don't offer the space, diversity and access and time for relaxation.

The River Derwent is Australia's deepest natural harbour and entices sailing in all weather. The safe port is not only a gateway to the southern seas and Antarctic exploration, but is also the finish line for one of the world's greatest ocean races, the Sydney to Hobart Yacht Race. The race for line honours concludes off Battery Point; the party continues on the docks of Hobart's historic waterfront well into the new year. Australia's largest food festival, the iconic Taste of Tasmania, feeds 250,000 ravenous patrons. A busy summer festival ensues, bringing Hobart to life and rivalling any port city in the world as a holiday season attraction.

Today's Hobart is in fact the third attempt at settlement. At the order of Governor King of New South Wales two new settlements were to be formed. The first was due to the serious concerns about the French inhabitation of Van Diemens Land. To combat this, in the spring of 1803 Governor King sent an ambitious 23-year-old naval officer, John Bowen, to the River Derwent with 49 settlers, convicts and military. The Derwent had already been chartered by Matthew Flinders' previous expedition, so Bowen followed those coordinates, landing at Risdon Cove on the eastern banks of the River Derwent on 12 September 1803. Meanwhile the experienced official who had formerly assisted in the establishment of the first fleet and its colonisation of Sydney was on his way from England with a far better stocked, prepared and skilled workforce of convicts, military and settlers. Lieutenant Governor David Collins was in charge of settling on the southern coast of New South Wales (now Victoria) in order to have a settlement near Bass Strait to protect that body of water from a potential invasion from the French navy.

Summer at Sandy Bay Beach

Winter sunset

Halfway through summer both settlements were without fresh water and struggling to grow crops in poor soil, and regular engagement with the indigenous people created an environment of fear.

Even with the advantages of fresh water, a deep harbour with safe anchorage, huge quantities of mature timber and a gentle lay of the land, establishing Hobart Town was indeed most challenging and unproductive.

TASMANIA

Government House, Hobart, Tas.

Hobart

FORGET ME NOT

By signs I cannot tell you.
How dear you are to me
My thoughts and words cannot describe
The love I feel for thee.

However, over that first summer, the hardships and troubles at both settlements would be great, and their successes few. Halfway through summer both settlements were without fresh water and struggling to grow crops in poor soil, and regular engagement with the indigenous people created an environment of fear. Governor Collins decided to disband the ill-fated attempt at Port Phillip Bay and headed for the River Derwent to join up with Lieutenant Bowen's settlement at Risdon Cove. Spending one night only on the eastern shore of the river, Collins and his officers took the advice of convict surveyor James Meehan and went in search of a more suitable location, and as a modern-day observer, you would have to admit they got it right. Although Bowen's 'Hobart' (Risdon) and Collins' 'Hobart' (Sullivans Cove) co-existed for a few months, causing great frustration to Governor King in Sydney, Bowen eventually resigned his position, allowing Governor Collins full authority. Both these settlements were named Hobart after Lord Hobart, Secretary of State for War and the Colonies.

Bowen left Van Diemens Land in August 1804, and sadly never returned. Even with the advantages of fresh water, a deep harbour with safe anchorage, huge quantities of mature timber and a gentle lay of the land, establishing Hobart Town was indeed most challenging and unproductive. Near starvation and a lack of facilities for its settlement meant that it remained little more than a camp, up until Collins' untimely death in March 1810. As a result, New South Wales Governor Lachlan Macquarie visited the island in 1811 to provide administration, and a series of interim governors took his direction.

MONA museum

4

Up until 1818 the convicts transported to Van Diemens Land were the re-offenders from Sydney, therefore skilled labour and model prisoners were not the order of the day.

By this time whaling had become the major industry in the town, employing over 500 seamen. Shipbuilding would soon also become a vital trade to supply seafarers and maritime workers. Up until 1818 the convicts transported to Van Diemens Land were the re-offenders from Sydney, therefore skilled labour and model prisoners were not the order of the day. The arrival of Governor William Sorell (1817-24) and Sir George Arthur (1824-36) provided order and administration and in 1825 Van Diemens Land would become self-governed and separate from New South Wales. A period of prosperity ensued for settlers and reformed convicts collectively, partially resulting from the export of fine wool, timber and wheat to colonies including the newly settled Western Australia and Victoria.

In 1837 Sir John and Lady Franklin arrived with a social conscience and refinement. This was in stark contrast to the previous governance of Governor Arthur, who had instituted projects such as the Port Arthur penitentiary, the Point Puer boys' prison, the Female Factory and a policy called the 'Black Line', the systematic removal of the indigenous inhabitants from the main island to Flinders Island in Bass Strait.

The 1850s would bring about massive changes for Hobart socially, psychologically and practically. These included the introduction of gas for lighting, the official renaming of Van Diemens Land to Tasmania, the cessation of convict transportation in 1853, the end of public execution, the near end of the southern right whaling industry and the first meeting of the House of Assembly at Parliament House. The British Redcoats certainly made a large impact on the culture and social scenes in Hobart up until their recall in 1870. The building boom in the 1860s included new cathedrals for the Anglican and Catholic faiths, the new Government House and Hobart's Town Hall. The 1870s saw the

Tasmanian Archives and Heritage Office, Hobart wharves 1930s

5

Stallholders at Salamanca Market

closure of the Female Factory in the Cascades, Port Arthur on the peninsula, the introduction of rail services, a new widespread fear of war and Hobart's preparations to defend itself against the Russians.

Hobart Town was declared a city in 1842 and changed its name to Hobart in 1881. 1893 would see the introduction of the first electric trams in the Southern Hemisphere, open-top double-deckers. At the turn of the century to mark federation, the Duke of York, the future king, visited Hobart; the new Customs House was opened; and soon after, the General Post Office. Hobart's maritime and general economy was on the move pre-WW1, as W.D. Peacock and H. Jones & Co's IXL took on the world in exporting fresh, and tinned fruit and numerous jams. On February 1954 Queen Elizabeth visited Hobart for the first time after her ascension to the throne, and unveiled the 150th anniversary memorial of the settlement of Hobart on Old Wharf.

Hobart also became the centre for Antarctic exploration. In 1911 Raoul Amundsen announced to the world his successful return from that continent from Hobart's GPO. Famous Hollywood heart-throb Errol Flynn was born at the Queen Alexandra Hospital in Battery Point in 1909, and with his fame, along with our new nickname 'The Apple Isle', Tasmania was well and truly on the map for reasons other than convicts. The last known thylacine died in 1936 at the Beaumaris Zoo on the Queens Domain. Drought and extreme temperatures caused the devastating bushfires of 1967 that destroyed over 1000 buildings and came to be known as the Black Tuesday fires. Within five hours, 652,000 acres were burned and there were 62 fatalities. In this same year trolley buses were removed as a form of public transport in a further attempt to conserve power.

An admirable attempt has now been made by the Hobart City Council to turn the city centre into a more pedestrian and bicycle friendly environment with the advent of the Elizabeth Street Mall, bicycle lanes, wider footpaths and the beautification of parks

Sunday Farm Gate Market, every sunday in Bathurst Street

and walks. Visitors flock to Hobart from interstate and overseas to the amazing MONA (Museum of Old and New Art) in Berriedale, north of Hobart. Along with its cultural festivals, it is creating a strong and diverse arts community.

While the story of Hobart's past is somewhat dark and sometimes violent, it provides an important connection and context to our fascinating built heritage, which is evident before you where ever you turn — you are able to visit so many of these iconic places within such a confined and convenient area. This city continues to captivate the interest of visitors and locals alike.

On February 1954 Queen Elizabeth visited Hobart for the first time after her ascension to the throne, and unveiled the 150th anniversary memorial of the settlement of Hobart on Old Wharf.

My HOBART

Warren Glover

It took a long time for me to ascertain that I was a sixth generation Hobartian, and even though I had the privilege of knowing two of my great grandparents, the more reticent culture they came from somewhat limited the sharing of their experiences.

These stories, though, are an important link to our colonial past and, bit by bit, I have been able to piece together the fascinating history of my family through the wonderful medium of storytelling, and the occasional discovery of a significant photograph or other relic. Mine is just one of the tens of thousands of accounts emanating from the island's early history, frequently including tales of tragedy not dissimilar to my family's own: infants that perished while travelling here by sea in the 1850s, other children placed in orphanages, a violent crime perpetrated in the family, a convict woman who married in Hobart even though she left a husband and children back in Glasgow, and a public divorce scandal dragged through the courts and newspapers with witness testimonies.

On the back of challenging experiences, though, descendants of the family enjoyed far more peaceful lives with strong bonds both in the family and tight-knit community. My mother often speaks of the many pleasant aspects of childhood in her time – the early swimming holes of Hobart, and the quiet streets where children would play happily with just a ball from morning to night, interrupted maybe twice in the day by an automobile, and more often by horse and carts, which were still common in the 1940s.

My father was an adventurer and thrill seeker, so his way of introducing me to local history was hands-on to say the least. In the 1970s, inner city Hobart had numerous historic homes that were sadly left derelict, some also having evidence of occupation by homeless persons. Whether it was in Hobart CBD, South Hobart, Battery Point or West Hobart, like a sheep to a shepherd I followed my dad as he explored all of these dilapidated spaces. We found many interesting and sometimes sad relics; on one occasion a man's entire worldly possessions in a shoebox on the floor next to a chair and an empty bottle of methylated spirits. My father's fine skills as a photographer and an eye for capturing both the new and the soon-to-be demolished, he made a strong impact on my mind and interest when it came to my sense of place, and the feeling that Hobart was my home.

In the 1970s my parents purchased a Victorian mansion (pictured) in Liverpool Street, the house of retired colonel John O'Boyle. When we moved in, the fittings were all in the lovely signature style of the sixties – oil heaters, lino floors, laminex panels, lime green paint and orange carpet – and the house reduced to a single storey.

My mother often speaks of the many pleasant aspects of childhood in her time – the early swimming holes of Hobart, and the quiet streets where children would play happily with just a ball from morning to night…

Author Warren Glover - founder of YouDo Hobart History, in front of family home in Liverpool Street.

8

One night we became very excited indeed as my endeavours were at last rewarded. 'Gold! Gold!' Inside a tobacco tin was a Bushell's tea packet containing flakes of gold amounting to $1000

When we examined the upstairs storey, we found that all the walls were whitewashed and featured hand-painted stencils, and the roof space contained treasures such as antique bottles, gilded picture frames and rolls of brail. But the biggest treasure of all we found out about from our new neighbour, Mrs Ward. 'Of course you know the legend of the house?' Legend! Dad's ears became very attentive. The legend was that the house had once been owned by a gold prospector who had hidden all his gold in the house as bricks. So my dad went quietly mad with gold fever, purchasing a metal detector, then spending the next couple of years climbing around foundations, crawl spaces, inside the roof and anywhere else he imagined the gold might be disclosed. When all other avenues appeared exhausted, I was sent up inside the chimneys, of which the house had plenty. One night we became very excited indeed as my endeavours were at last rewarded. 'Gold! Gold!' Inside a tobacco tin was a Bushell's tea packet containing flakes of gold amounting to $1000, a considerable amount at that time. A party ensued, and my dad renewed his hunt with zeal. Watching my parents work so hard together in returning the grand house to something like the way the Colonel had intended was so very exciting. In rolled the antiques with which to fit it out – Pears soap prints, brass beds and tall boys.

Skipping forward 20 years, now married with two small children, I received an excellent suggestion – why not spend time developing a hobby around something I am passionate about? The first thing that came to mind was our wonderful Hobart story and the beautiful remnant of heritage buildings from the Georgian period onwards that could be found all around the city.

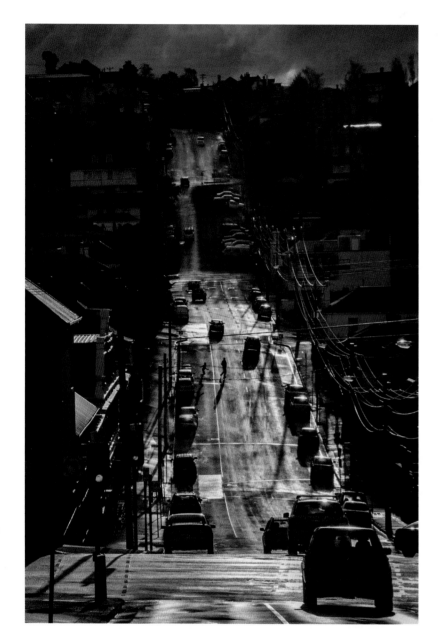

I became a regular fixture at the Tasmaniana Library in Hobart, went on every tour available, spent hours poring over the numerous excellent Hobart history books on offer and took advantage of whatever I could find to gain enough knowledge to be able to start telling our story myself. In 2003 I started Flashback Tours, four-hour tours in a fully licensed car with catering and classical music, and showed people from all over the world around our remarkable city.

In 2007 I started working for the Henry Jones Art Hotel. Originally employed as a concierge, I was later approached by the general manager with an idea for a new and somewhat unusual role – history liaison. For four wonderful years I engaged with travellers about the rich tale of Sir Henry Jones, the buildings that make up the hotel and its surrounds, and introduced guests to the possibility of convict ancestry with a list of convicts sharing their surname. I also took guests on regular tours of Hobart, and on a weekly occasion had the privilege of sharing in the outstanding art and history tour, which I never grew tired of. Explaining and bringing to life our human story became a daily thrill for me, and certainly something I wanted to continue both as a career and a personal passion. So in 2014 I started to create my current business venture as an independent operator. *YouDo Hobart History* enables me to engage in a variety of activities, acting as an author, a public speaker and a consultant. Daily tours tell the story of how Hobart grew from the humblest beginnings and follow it through every stage of its incredible past, endeavouring to stir up the imaginations of people and to bring context to their Tasmanian experience. Every day my passion for Hobart grows. I hope this introduction to some of Hobart's iconic buildings and places also incites your desire to discover Hobart more fully.

I became a regular fixture at the Tasmaniana Library in Hobart, went on every tour available, spent hours poring over the numerous excellent Hobart history books on offer

PHOTOGRAPHING *on the streets of Hobart*

Paul County

Photography came to Van Diemens Land not long after its invention in 1839. It was popular in Tasmania, with an affluent and well-established element in the population. In 1843 G.B. Goodman, Australia's first professional photographer, opened a studio in the then Hobarton. He produced tiny daguerreotypes, popular with those who wanted a memento to give to loved ones — it was a long and often lonely journey by sea to the mainland or London.

Daguerreotypes were small, expensive and unable to be reproduced, so only portraiture was practised to any degree. Due to long exposure times, neck braces were often used to hold the sitter's head still!

From October to December 1848, J.W. Newland from Sydney was in Hobart Town advertising photographic portrait miniatures in morocco cases for a guinea each from his Daguerrean Gallery above Miss Hedger's shop in the Stone Buildings, Murray Street *(see page 81).*

From his studio window early in December, Newland took Australia's earliest surviving streetscape, a whole-plate daguerreotype of Hobart Town showing the public buildings in Murray Street, the wharf and a corner of the old gaol (reproduced on opposite page). It is now in the TMAG, still in its original Huon pine frame. Newland's image gives us a glimpse of the past looking down Murray Street to Battery Point and the wharves and shows people and horse-drawn cabs in the street, whaling ships at the New Wharf [later Princes Wharf] and the old gaol. During this period, public executions were still carried out. Often crowds of up to 2,500 gathered to watch.

11

Old Hobart - Showing
Goal corner of which
public execution took place

J.W. Newland (1810-1857), Murray Street, 1848 Daguerreotype full plate, copper, silver, timber

Image Courtesy: Tasmanian Museum and Art Gallery

From his studio window early in December,
Newland took Australia's earliest surviving streetscape

On occasions I felt I was channelling Newland and some of my other favourite Hobart photographers: Frank Bolt (my favourite is his classic 1981 book, *Old Hobart Town Today*); Frank Hurley, an Australian photographer and adventurer who when based in Hobart participated in a number of photographic expeditions to Antarctica; and John Watt Beattie. Beattie probably did more than anyone to shape the accepted visual image of Tasmania. An admirer of William Piguenit, Beattie stressed the same wildly romantic aspects of the island's beauty. His photography included framed prints, postcards, lantern-slides and albums, and was the basis for a popular and pleasing set of Tasmanian pictorial stamps (in print from 1899 to 1912).

....

the sun pokes through in shards, blinding drivers commuting to work along Sandy Bay Road

....

Hobart is so picturesque, especially in autumn with its golden hues. It's a photographer's paradise. The glorious river, the often snow-capped Mount Wellington making a lovely backdrop, the charming cottages of Battery Point — it sometimes feels almost clichéd.

One frosty 2°C winter morning at 7am I was transfixed when the sun rising over the eastern shore hit the highest peak of Mount Wellington first and it glowed orange.

In winter the sky can become dark grey and bubbling, providing a moody backdrop and dramatic lighting when the sun pokes through in shards, blinding drivers commuting to work along Sandy Bay Road. The trees drop their leaves and the full detail of buildings is revealed and the sun tracks across the sky on a lower arc. Around 4pm a warming winter sun can stream down Hobart's north-facing streets — then those travelling home north along the Brooker Highway get blinded.

And don't be afraid to photograph into the sun — just adjust your camera metering and bracket your images in the manual setting. Some streets and facades of some buildings never receive full sun, so they can be photographed back-lit.

There is no right or wrong time or season to photograph but as a rule many photographers shoot early and late in the day. Most of the images in this book were taken between 6 and 10am or 3 and 8pm, depending on the season. This is when the light is softer, warmer and the shadows longest.

One frosty 2°C winter morning at 7am I was transfixed when the sun rising over the eastern shore hit the highest peak of Mount Wellington first and it glowed orange. Then the light gradually crept up along the long, parallel-running Davey and Macquarie streets, gently kissing the hand-chiselled cornices of the glorious Georgian buildings — shimmering like gold dust on an angel's wing. Ten minutes later it hit St Joseph's Church and it also glowed.

Look up in Hobart and you will often be amazed. Don't pack up when it rains… after rain the streets shimmer and reflect shapes and lights, often with interesting results.

14

*Look up in Hobart
and you will
often be amazed.*

15

Walch Optics in Macquarie Street and Stallards Camera House in
Elizabeth Street Mall are Hobart's oldest camera stores and are there
to offer expert advice.

Photography can be a life-long learning experience. Take your time
and enjoy the journey.

References and further reading:

C Long, *Tasmanian Photographers 1840-1940*, Hobart, 1995

Frank Bolt, *Old Hobart Town Today*, 1981

Nick Hogarth, *The Wild Ride*, 1989

The Companion to Tasmanian History

www.utas.edu.au/library/companion_to_tasmanian_history/P/Photography.htm

www.kenrockwell.com and www.dpreview.com are two of my favourite websites.

16

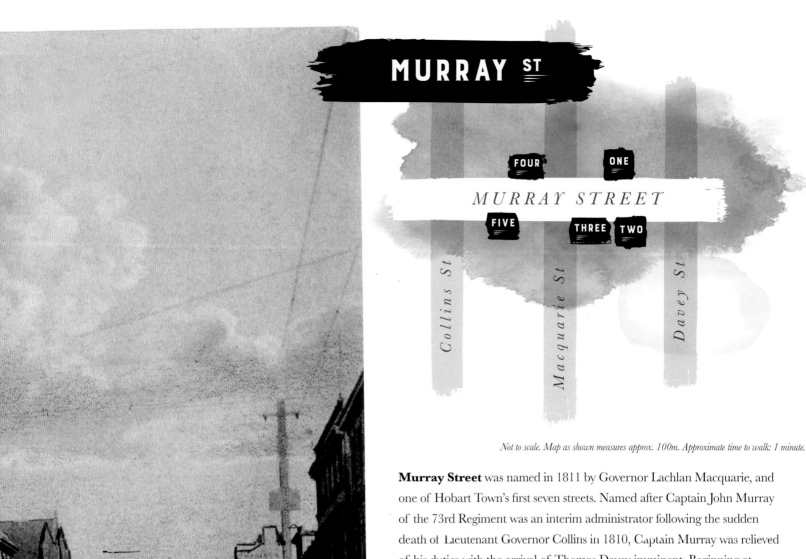

MURRAY ST

MURRAY STREET

FOUR · ONE

FIVE · THREE · TWO

Collins St

Macquarie St

Davey St

Not to scale. Map as shown measures approx. 100m. Approximate time to walk: 1 minute.

Murray Street was named in 1811 by Governor Lachlan Macquarie, and one of Hobart Town's first seven streets. Named after Captain John Murray of the 73rd Regiment was an interim administrator following the sudden death of Lieutenant Governor Collins in 1810, Captain Murray was relieved of his duties with the arrival of Thomas Davey imminent. Beginning at Waterman's Dock, flanked by Customs House Hotel and Parliament House. Murray Street then rises to the city centre to pass the original Court House (MU *one*), the site of the old gaol where public executions were conducted diagonally across from the Cathedral (MU *four*) before crossing the Hobart Town Rivulet now beneath the street.

MURRAY STREET, LOOKING SOUTH, HOBART.

MU ONE | **State Treasury Buildings** | *21 Murray Street, Hobart*

This u-shaped complex constructed in several phases in smooth dressed stone is now a united series, but originally all buildings were designed to have an independent purpose. Designed by civil engineer and architect John Lee Archer, although not completed until after his dismissal in 1842. The building to the right housed the convict and police department's administration. To the left, on the corner of Macquarie Street in the colony's first courthouse, opening just 10 days earlier than its counterpart in Sydney, importantly now enabling the colony to dispense justice locally. This series of buildings has an elegant charm, creating a dramatic impact on the streetscape and surrounds.

Did You Know?

'Hobart has a peculiarity – it is the neatest town that the sun shines on, and I incline to believe it is also the cleanest.' These were the words of great American writer Mark Twain, who was favourably impressed during his visit in 1895. He continued, 'The voyage up the Derwent displays a grand succession of fairy visions in its entire length elsewhere unequalled.'

MU TWO

Savings Bank

26 Murray Street,
Hobart

The Savings Bank was largely
a philanthropic institution, at the
insistence of George Washington
Walker, to improve the lot of
the town's working class. Fifteen
thousand accounts were opened
in the first dozen years. At its
completion the cost of construction
was 4,349 pounds in 1859. Built
with white freestone from Kangaroo
Point, the commercial building has
a notable interior, as its banking
chamber is rather spectacular and
designed at a later date by Architects
Walker and Johnston, the building
Architect was Edward Rowntree.

Did You Know?

*The last hanging at the
Hobart Penitentiary Gaol
was as recent as 1946.*

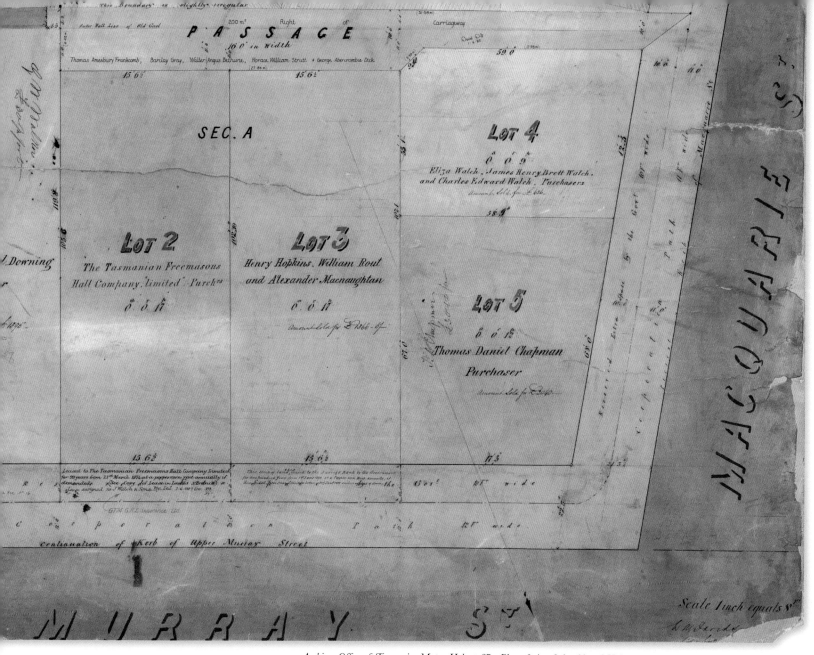

Archives Office of Tasmania: Map - Hobart 67 - Plan of site of the old gaol Hobart - surveyor W M Davidson, AF394-1-66

 **MU THREE**

Derwent & Tamar Insurance Building

28 Murray Street, Hobart

Another of Architect Henry Hunter's grand Victoria building designs, completed in 1877 upon the former Hobart Town Gaol site, where the gallows stood and operated for approximately forty years. Constructed of fine white stone, featuring polished granite columns, basement level with light well, iron railing and large stone posts, also visible are rounded corner windows.

DERWENT & TAMAR

GS BANK

Far right building: Derwent & Tamar Insurance Building
Middle building: Savings Bank

St. David's Cathedral
23 Murray Street, Hobart

The first primitive church built over the burial place of Lieutenant Governor Collins blew down in a storm. The initial stone church on Murray Street however dominated the town's skyline until its demolition in 1875. The construction of this cathedral was achieved in three stages between 1868 and 1936. The tower is a city landmark, with a full compliment of bells and built with Oatlands sandstone. With much celebration and ceremony the church was named St. David's after the forefather of the colony, Governor Collins, and although Collins was an accomplished administrator, his suitability of having the church named after him was never called into question. Collins, not travelling with his wife, had numerous extra-marital affairs while in Hobart Town, in full public view.

MU FIVE Hadley's Orient Hotel

34 Murray Street, Hobart

This grand hotel of Hobart has stood proudly, and been an industry innovator, for over 175 years. Having the installation of electric lights, a telephone on every floor, and the first elevator of any hotel in the country. A former licensee and owner Mr John Webb, an ex-convict as so many entrepreneurs in town were, was indeed an interesting character. He patented an ice-freezing machine, allowing him to have an ice-skating rink in the hotel, which would later become the ballroom. Webb had his own icehouse on Mount Wellington, and engaged regularly by horseback in retrieving ice in large blocks for use at his establishment.

26

Did You Know?

George Adams, who instituted the first Tattersall Lottery in 1895, offered Hadley's Orient Hotel as second prize. Fortunately this questionable lottery failed.

All images Hadley's Orient Hotel

28

Murray Street - Architectural Features

31

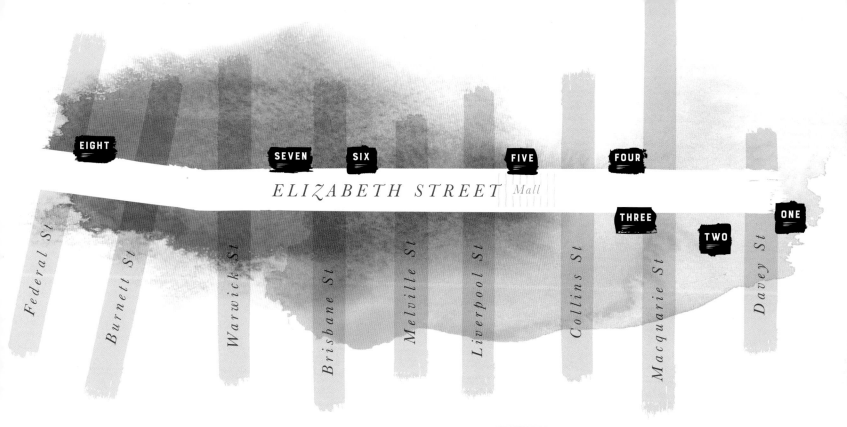

EIGHT SEVEN SIX FIVE FOUR

ELIZABETH STREET Mall

THREE TWO ONE

Federal St

Burnett St

Warwick St

Brisbane St

Melville St

Liverpool St

Collins St

Macquarie St

Davey St

Not to scale. Map as shown measures approx. 1.8km. Approximate time to walk: 25 minutes.

ELIZABETH ST

Beginning at the white gateposts of Government House (demolished in 1858) Elizabeth Street was the main road or highway from the seat of governance located at the regal reserve on the intersection of Macquarie Street. The street was named after the wife of then Governor of New South Wales, Lachlan Macquarie. When visiting Van Diemens Land for the first time in 1811, Macquarie assigned surveyor James Meehan the task of marking out the first seven streets of Hobart Town, of which Elizabeth Street was one. From then on Elizabeth Street was the principal road for goods and services transported to New Norfolk and Launceston, including the English-style coach system. Suburbs and districts springing from this road include New Town, Moonah, O'Briens Bridge (now Glenorchy), Montrose and the central midlands towns and settlements of Kempton, Oatlands, Ross, Campbell Town and Perth.

32

Hobart City Council Building

16 Elizabeth Street,
Hobart

During the 20th century the Hydro Electric Commission invested heavily in Tasmania's natural environment, bringing economic benefits to the state as well as creating jobs. Tasmania would go on to become a world leader in the production of hydro electricity. The stunning corner building on the intersection of Elizabeth and Davey streets is one of the state's finest contributions to Art Deco architecture. Built by the Hydro Electric Commission in 1938, and kept illuminated at night, it quickly became an icon of the new wave, suggesting energy and modernity among Hobart's streetscape of abundant Georgian, Regency and Victorian architecture. In the 1990s, the Hydro Electric Commission was accommodated in new premises behind its original building, which now housed the Hobart City Council, meaning only one letter in the acronym (HEC) needed changing.

34

Franklin Square

| *Franklin Square*

Franklin Square is named after former Governor of Van Diemens Land, Sir John Franklin. Sir John was knighted prior to his appointment as the heir apparent to the newly departed Governor George Arthur. An imposing bronze statue is the central feature of the park bearing his name. When finding out that this very statue was being erected in England to honour the exploratory career of Sir John, the government of the day enacted the purchase of a replica for Hobart Town's first garden park. The square and Hobart Town Hall were home to the original Government House before its demolition in 1858. Georges Square, situated at the western end of the original Government House, was the site of regular musters as far back as 1817. During the Second World War, the park was used as a central Hobart air raid shelter; therefore the removal of fine iron mongery was seen as a practical step, allowing easier access. However, one piece still remains today *(see below)*.

Colonial Mutual Life Building

18 Elizabeth Street,
Hobart

Colonial Mutual Life Assurance Association Society Limited was formed in Melbourne in 1873. Further investment and expansion in between the two world wars saw CML align its series of new buildings throughout South East Asia and South Africa to Australian architectural firm Hennessey & Hennessey. Jack F Hennessey Junior is regarded as Australia's first international architect. Hobart's CML building, erected in 1936, offers trademark Hennessey signatures, with classic Gothic Art Deco – in a way a small-scale Manhattan offering – sensibly in context with Hobart's then low rise street compliance. Multi-coloured terracotta tiles, gargoyles and an interesting finish in pink granite (brought from Queensland and previously not used in Hobart) created a one-off for Hobart buildings.

Did You Know?

Hobart's foundry industry was of a very high standard. Numerous fine examples remain in Hobart, including the Botanical Gardens entrance gates (QD three) and the synagogue (ARG four). A six-foot high iron railing with proud gates and posts surrounds.

EZ FOUR Hobart GPO

| Hobart GPO

This Edwardian Baroque-style building is Hobart's fourth official post office, a dignified and unpretentious building that has the same Westminster chime as Big Ben of London. The clock tower is in alignment with Elizabeth rather than Macquarie Street, and is protected from the weather by a semi-circle pediment carried on brackets. Designed by architect Alan Walker, and funded by the people of Hobart in celebration of Federation, the building was opened in September 1905; a telephone exchange was added two years later. The Hobart GPO's most heralded moment came on March 7, 1912, when internationally renowned Antarctic explorer Roald Amundsen telegraphed to the world that he had reached the South Pole and returned safely.

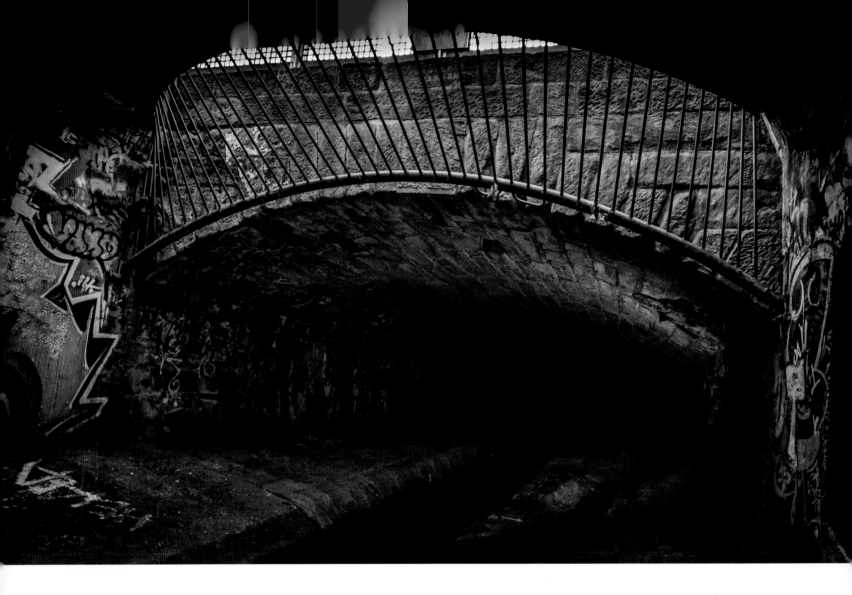

EZ FIVE | **Wellington Bridge** | *Elizabeth Street Mall, Hobart*

Every street in Hobart Town running in the north to south line had to have a timber, brick or stone bridge crossing the Hobart Rivulet, enabling the continuation of each street while maintaining the flow of the rivulet to the nearby Derwent River. Many of these early bridges were under severe pressure from the flooding that occurred when Mount Wellington had consecutive days of rain or snow melt.

This version of Wellington Bridge is in fact the fourth built before 1841. The distance by road from Hobart to Launceston was calculated from this landmark. It can now be seen through a viewing portal in the Elizabeth Street Mall; previously it could only be viewed through the tunnel that now incorporates the original rivulet stream.

EZ SIX | Island Espresso | *173 Elizabeth Street, Hobart*

Today one of Hobart's longest serving cafes may well be one of Hobart's oldest surviving buildings. The brick section at the rear is an early cottage dating to approximately 1814, as the street grid was marked out by that time, though not properly excavated. Inside the Espresso Bar is a rare building technique called 'nogging', which involved the filling in of timber studs with brick. This may be the only surviving example in Hobart. The front section, built of timber, was added when the building was converted to a business in the 1830s.

 **Westella** | *181 Elizabeth Street, Hobart*

This three-storey, late Georgian mansion was built in 1835 for Henry Hopkins, the first wool exporter in the new colony. It originally featured a croquet lawn, summer houses and numerous bathrooms. This merchant and philanthropist's home features the finest fittings: cornices, timber balustrades, fanlights and an Ionic portico. Of course, Mr Hopkins and family didn't spend their summers in the bustling town, preferring instead to enjoy the warmer months at their appropriately named 'Summerhome' just five miles north of Westella. Due to the absence of a town hall until 1869, the Governor's orders and proclamations were made from the porch of Westella – announcements included the death of King William, the birth of Prince Edward, Queen Victoria's accession to the throne and the cessation of convict transportation, a development in which Henry Hopkins played a part.

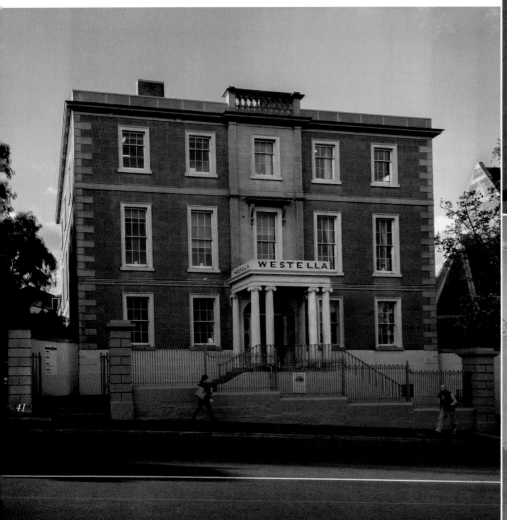

State Cinema | *375 Elizabeth Street, North Hobart*

The State Cinema, an Art Deco classic, is a survivor of Hobart's 20th century night-life entertainment boom. Right up until the early 1960s Hobart was busy with cinema, dance halls, live theatre and clubs. The State Cinema survived the trends that followed, such as the 'drive-in', television, mainstream cinema and home entertainment, and now is an institution and icon of Hobart culture. It houses not only its original movie theatre, but seven other more intimate cinemas, as well as an innovative rooftop cinema. The State Cinema was originally called the 'Picture Palace', which had the advantage of the North Hobart orchestra to accompany its films.

42

43

Elizabeth Street - Architectural Features

Tasmanian Archives and Heritage Office

ARGYLE ST

This street was named by Governor Lachlan Macquarie on his visit in 1811, after the county Argyle in Scotland, the county of his origin.

45

FIVE   FOUR THREE   TWO

ARGYLE STREET

ONE

Brisbane St

Melville St

Bathurst St

Liverpool St

Collins St

Macquarie St

Davey St

Not to scale. Map as shown measures approx 650m. Approximate time to walk: 8 minutes.

Carnegie Library Building

| 16 Argyle Street, Hobart

Mr Andrew Carnegie, an established multi-millionaire from America, was, at the turn of the century, extending his philanthropic kindness to all of the colonies by supplying the bricks and mortar for library projects, as long as sound business acumen was proven, and books and the appropriate land provided. In the case of Hobart, once Mr Carnegie had gained those assurances and knowledge of the land available behind the Town Hall, he proceeded with a donation of £7,500. This magnificent offer was referred to as a 'God out of a machine'. The library was completed in 1904 and is a good example of the Classical Revival style. Today it houses the Maritime Museum, offering a sample of our very rich maritime history, with a diverse and interesting collection.

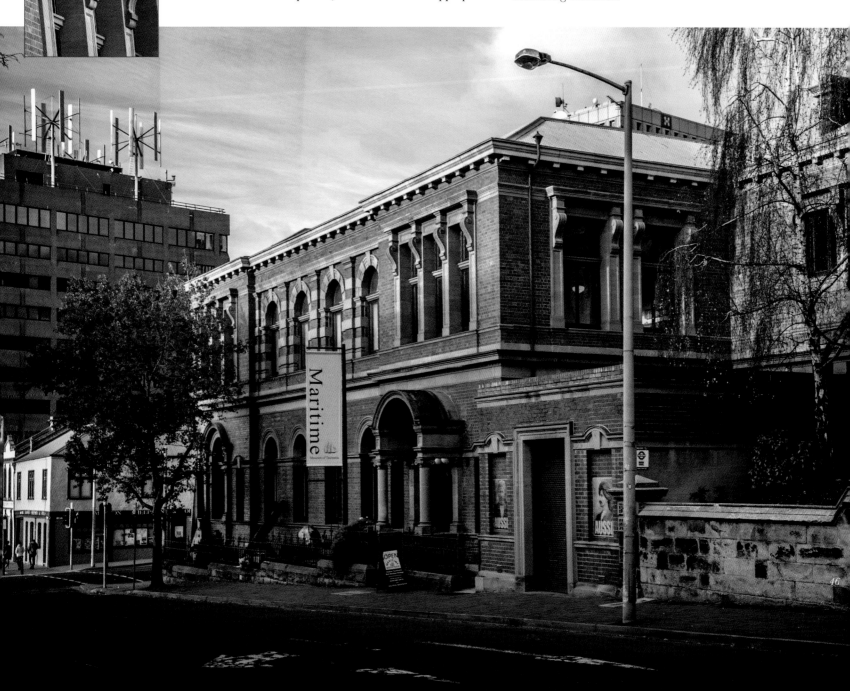

ARG TWO

Tasmanian Museum Gallery Building

| *Dunn Place*

This building was another in the golden era of architect Henry Hunter. It displays beautifully executed stone detailing. His drawings were awarded first place in the contest to design the Royal Society Museum and Art Gallery, in which he entered under the pseudonym 'Nimrod'. The first stage was completed in 1862; the second stage, opened to the public in 1889, ran from the Royal Society Museum entrance down Argyle Street towards the waterfront.

Did You Know?

Daylight saving was introduced in Tasmania in 1967 to reduce power usage after a drought and the resulting 'Black Tuesday' bushfires. From then on, the rest of Australia followed, except for Queensland.

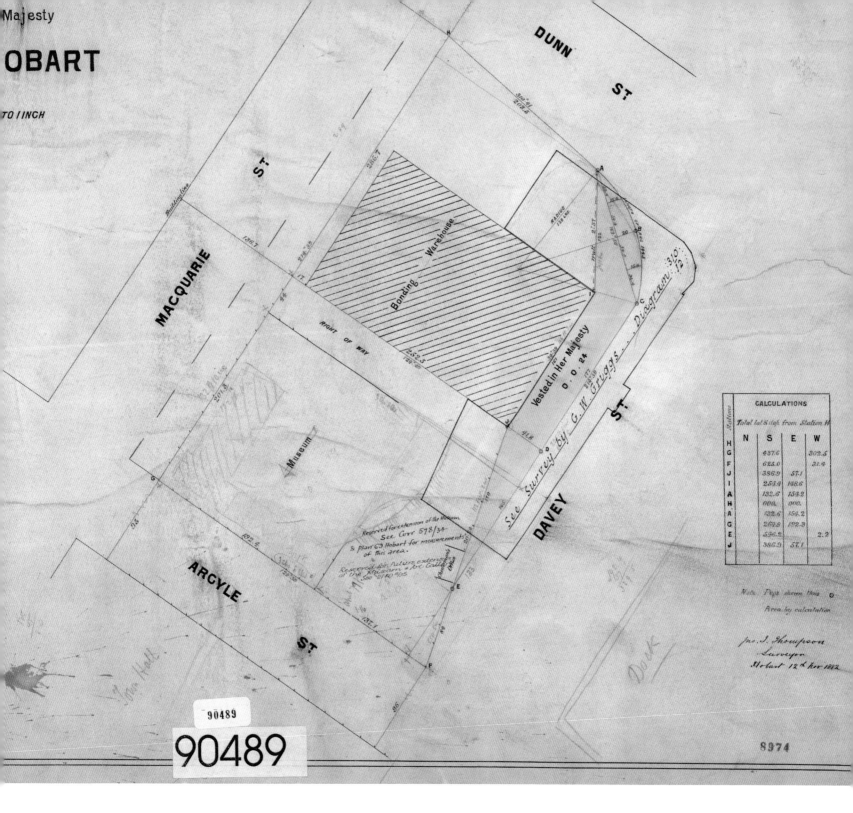

Map - Hobart 84 - Plan showing Museum and Bonding Warehouse,
Hobart - surveyor John T Thompson AF394-1-84

ARG THREE — Temple House | *55 Argyle Street, Hobart*

Built in approximately 1824, Temple House is one of the finest complete Georgian townhouses in Australia. It boasts a cantilevered staircase, and a storied basement that got the building's owners into a fair amount of strife, their having been mentioned nine times in court in regard to its use for illegal spirits trading. Judah and Joseph Solomon arrived in Van Diemen's Land as convicts in 1819, and by the late 1830s had over thirty properties in their portfolio. The brothers were prominent members of the Jewish Congregation that worshipped in their home, hence the name 'Temple House'. So wealthy by now, they chose to donate a portion of their garden for the building of Hobart Town's own synagogue (ARG *four*).

 **ARG FOUR**

Hobart Synagogue | *59 Argyle Street, Hobart*

Only in Hobart could you have a Jewish synagogue designed by an ex-convict Scotsman in Egyptian Revival style. Australia's earliest synagogue opened in 1845. Prior to that the Hebrew congregation worshipped at the home of Judah Solomon, Temple House (ARG *three*). Designed in the most elegant fashion by architect James Thomson, the building is recessed behind a fine example of a Hobart Town foundry. A fluted cornice is one of many unique external features of this internationally significant building. In the interior are decorative elements representing plants and Egyptian motifs, and the chandelier was locally crafted. The Hebrew inscription above the front door states 'Wherever my name is mentioned there I will come to you and bless you.'

אנכי ה לא תרצח
לא יהיה לא תנאף
לא תשא לא תגנב
זכור את לא תענה
כבד את לא תחמד

דע לפני מי אתה עומד

All images Hobart Synagogue

ARG FIVE | Hobart Fire Brigade | *79-85 Argyle Street, Hobart*

In June 1910 the superintendent recommended a new brigade headquarters. In consequence, some of the earlier buildings were demolished to make room while others were initially retained. Eventually the tender process for the new building was accepted and, at a cost of £2,669, builder Jas. McKenzie commenced work. A further extension in 1925 to the brigade's head station was designed by architect R.F. Richards and included a gymnasium and seven flats for married staff.

Argyle Street - Architectural Features

HARRINGTON ST

Harrington Street commemorates the Earl of Harrington, one of Lachlan Macquarie's commanders. It was one of the principal streets laid out in Hobart Town in 1811.

HARRINGTON STREET

ONE

TWO

Patrick St

Brisbane St

Melville St

Bathurst St

Liverpool St

Not to scale. Map as shown measures approx. 400m. Approximate time to walk: 5 minutes.

HOBART FROM NORTH No I

Tasmanian Archives and Heritage Office

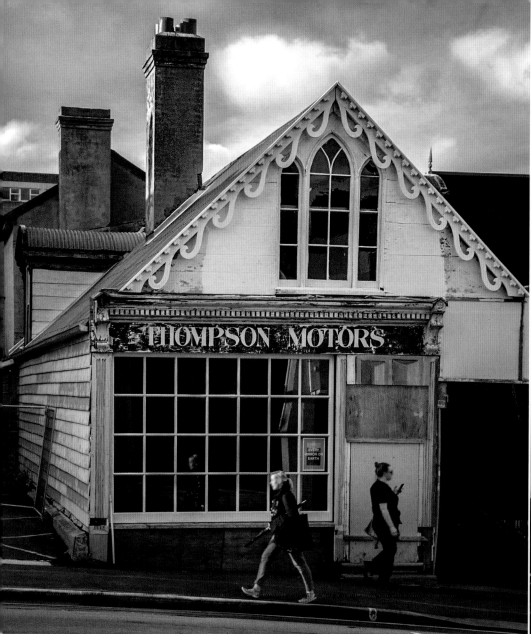

Gothic Shop and Residence | *121 Harrington Street, Hobart*

This is one of the few surviving timber buildings that remain in Hobart's central business district. Built in approximately 1840, it served as both a shop front and residence. In the last forty years this building has had more than its fair share of knocks – arson attacks, graffiti, roof leaks, squatters, and a disgruntled local minority wanting the derelict eyesore demolished. Thankfully its owners have faithfully and lovingly restored this rare specimen for Hobartians and visitors alike to enjoy.

Did You Know?

Silver Top Taxis began humbly in Hobart Town in 1843 as Broughton Horse Cabs. Broughton's horse-drawn cabs were a regular feature in Hobart's streets even after the popular introduction of the motor vehicle. Father Christmas was always transported into Hobart during the Christmas trading period in a Broughton's horse-drawn cab.

56

HA TWO · St. Mary's Cathedral | *180 Harrington Street, Hobart*

For some time members of the Catholic faith in Hobart were unable to build their cathedral. In 1868, however, due to a donation of £10,000 by Mr Roderic O'Connor, they were able to build on the outer fringe of Hobart. Unfortunately, during construction, a storm caused grave damage to the tower. This tower rose 100 feet above street level and was decorated with panels and gilt cornices, and framed by four central arches. Upon inspection in 1872, large stones supporting the tower were found to be unsteady and therefore creating a structural weakness. Henry Hunter, famed local architect, opted for the course of dismantling the entire tower. During this time the weight and pressure undermined the entire structure. The conclusion was that the short-lived cathedral had to be closed. Henry Hunter's rebuilt cathedral had a soft opening in July 1878 with its first wedding ceremony.

Harrington Street - Architectural Features

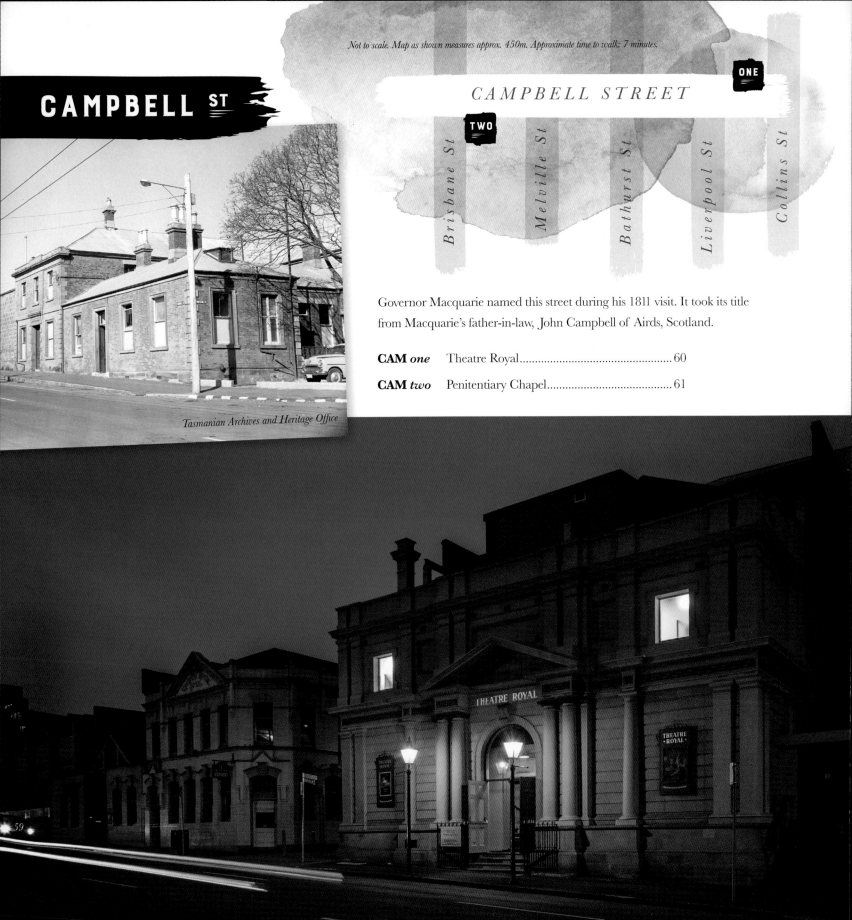

CAMPBELL ST

CAMPBELL STREET

ONE

TWO

Brisbane St

Melville St

Bathurst St

Liverpool St

Collins St

Governor Macquarie named this street during his 1811 visit. It took its title from Macquarie's father-in-law, John Campbell of Airds, Scotland.

Tasmanian Archives and Heritage Office

THEATRE ROYAL

THEATRE ROYAL

THEATRE ROYAL

59

Theatre Royal | *29 Campbell Street, Hobart*

The Theatre Royal is Australia's oldest theatre and is still in operation. It opened its doors in 1837 courtesy of the enterprises of Peter DeGraves of the Cascade Brewery (SoHo *one*). In the 19th century the theatre was located in the infamous district of Wapping; during this time it was nicknamed 'Satan's Synagogue', largely due to the cramped, smelly conditions and lowbrow entertainment. The façade of the theatre is a later addition designed by ex-convict James Thomson, and the rough external sidewalls of the original building remain visible. The acoustics are a notable feature, with a whisper on stage carrying up to the gods. After an almost totally devastating fire in 1984, extensive renovations have gifted the old theatre a phenomenal finish and renewed comfort for performers and audience members.

Did You Know?

Charles Blondin was a hero of the Victorian era, a household name before the advent of film and the mass media. Blondin, a Frenchman, tightrope walked across Niagara Falls while pushing a woman in a wheelbarrow. When he performed at the Theatre Royal, to promote his act and sell tickets he tightrope walked across Campbell Street to the Sir George Arthur Hotel from the theatre roof, while blindfolded.

CAM TWO

Penitentiary Chapel | *Corner Campbell and Brisbane Streets, Hobart*

It was once said, 'Sir Christopher Wren designed no more beautiful church than this one'. With its Renaissance tower, it is one of the finest examples of its kind in Australia, and probably the finest work of John Lee Archer (built 1831-33). The entire Prisoners' Barracks began in Brisbane Street and ran two city blocks down Campbell Street to Bathurst Street. Sadly, this building complex was demolished in the 1960s due to the new prison opening at Risdon Vale. The Penitentiary Chapel has housed not only a chapel, law courts, exercise yard, early gunpowder magazine and solitary confinement cells, but also an execution yard with gallows, still in working order, where hangings were carried out right up until 1946. Today, 'The Tench', named by the convicts previously housed therein, is an incredible colonial exhibit run by the National Trust, which offers four tours daily and is an absolute must-see for anyone remotely interested in Hobart's history.

62

63

A·D·1925

EXCHANGE

1870

JOHN BLUNDSTONE & SON

LIMITED

MACQUARIE ST

Van Diemens Land was under the administration of New South Wales up until 1825, during which time Governor Lachlan Macquarie visited several times. Following the sudden death of Governor David Collins in 1810, Macquarie came to inspect how the fledgling colony had progressed. Upon that inspection he was most unhappy that it was so haphazard in its layout; most of the convict-built cottages were centred upon the rivulet. Travelling with Macquarie was ex-convict surveyor James Meehan, who marked out each of the seven initial streets. Macquarie Street was one of these. The street's accessibility and broadness is due to the principle of allowing enough space for a gun carriage, potentially pulled by up to ten bullocks, to be able to do a u-turn.

Tasmanian Archives and Heritage Office

MACQUARIE ST LOOKING S FROM CATHEDRAL, HOBART.   240.B.   BEATTIE, HOBART

FOURTEEN THIRTEEN TWELVE TEN EIGHT SIX FIVE FOUR TWO

Market Pl

MACQUARIE STREET

ELEVEN NINE SEVEN THREE ONE

Harrington St *Murray St* *Elizabeth St* *Argyle St* *Campbell St* *Evans St*

Did You Know?

On April Fool's Day 1955, parking meters began operating in Hobart, the first in any capital city in the country. Thirty-one tickets were given on that first day.

Not to scale. Map as shown measures approx. 1.2km. Approximate time to walk: 20 minutes.

MAC ONE Gasworks

| *2 Macquarie Street, Hobart*

The Hobart Gas Company's timing was impeccable — with whale numbers severely depleted after half a century of that unconstrained industry, the introduction of gas was very well received. Fifty miles of gas mains were installed underground throughout the city. Experienced industry workers emigrated from Scotland and coal was processed to produce the gas. The common thought was that with the illumination of Hobart's streets, night crime was sure to diminish. The Gas Company was formed in 1854 at a public meeting. Eventually though, the demand for electricity led to the company's discontinuation in 1978.

 MAC TWO **Hobart City Hall** | *57-63 Macquarie Street, Hobart*

Hobart City Hall stands on the former site of the City Markets building, which was destroyed by the 1890 Wapping district fires. For many years it served as Hobart's largest entertainment venue, and is still frequently used for concerts, festivals and exhibitions. The 70-foot high ceiling is pressed tin and the hall has a venue capacity of 3,200 people. Elements of the building express a strong link to the Arts and Crafts period.

69

The list of the various uses and acts the City Hall has been home to is a source of amusement and of note:

~ Screening of the film 'For The Term Of His Natural Life' in 1933 for a short season

~ Tattersalls Cash Draw

~ The White Stripes 2006

~ Australian Basketball Championships 1949

~ Skyhooks 1975

~ Andre the Giant and numerous wrestling bouts

~ Miss Australia ceremony 1971

~ Don McLean

~ AC/DC 1976, 77

~ Warehouse for military equipment WW2

Commissariat Store | *Dunn Place*

This was the first substantial government building in the colony, replacing the largely redundant store on Hunter Island. The bricks for this building were fired locally in 1808, and the store was fully operational by 1810. It was originally a large brick box with one door on the ground floor, so only one Redcoat was needed to guard its all-important contents, which were feeding and clothing 70 per cent of the colony. It is the oldest building in Hobart's central business district, and boasts being the longest continuously occupied building in Australia. In 1811, when surveyor James Meehan was assigned by Governor Lachlan Macquarie the task of laying out the initial grid of Hobart Town's streets, Macquarie Street was the principal street that ran from the face of the Commissariat Store, adding further provenance to this important historic building.

The Hope and Anchor

| *65 Macquarie Street, Hobart*

The first tavern on this location was a single-storey timber premises, named the Hope Inn, in 1807. The tavern clearly couldn't have a better position at the time: to the right was the Hobart Rivulet and directly in front was the sandy beach of Sullivans Cove. Later in the 1820s it became a more substantial two-storey brick hotel, an established hotel in the town, and has been known as the Hope and Anchor for over a century.

Ingle Hall | *Corner Argyle and Macquarie Street, Hobart*

This superb example of a Georgian townhouse is perhaps the finest of its kind in any city in the country. Dated around 1814, it was built on land granted to wealthy landowner Edward Lord. John Ingle, the house's builder, was a grazier and merchant, and considering the rather prestigious location of his home – on a main corner, in the main street opposite the Regal Reserve – was a man of great business acumen. Ingle Hall also operated as an inn, a museum, and the initial home of the Hutchins School.

Did You Know?

The actor's actor, Sir Laurence Olivier, and Vivien Leigh performed at the Theatre Royal in the play 'The School For Scandal' in June 1948. Sir Laurence was most taken with the theatre. 'We appreciate playing here not only because it is a beautiful little theatre; it is more than that. Your parents and grandparents have sat in the audience. It has built up atmosphere and the secret to atmosphere is antiquity – don't let it go.'

MAC SIX

Mercury Building

93 Macquarie Street,
Hobart

From small beginnings: In 1854 George Jones and ex-convict John Davies started the *Hobarton Mercury* in a modest little building on this location; in 1902 a modern, new building was completed. A Goss rotary press arrived from Chicago weighing 25 tons in that year. In 1940 this landmark Art Deco office and printery were built; this and Ingle Hall next door (MAC *five*) were used by the *Mercury* until offered for sale in 2012. The *Mercury* now operates out of modern offices in Salamanca Square, with printing facilities in the city's north.

Did You Know?

In 1839 Edward Abbott founded the Hobart Town Advertiser. *Abbott went on to publish Australia's first cookbook in 1864. Titled* The English and Australian Cookery Book. Cookery for the Many, as Well as for the "Upper Ten Thousand", *it was a gastronomic miscellany of 'the modern cookery of the mother country and the colonies', and of Continental and Hebrew cookery. Recipes included 'Roast Beef of Old England', 'Kangaroo Steamer' and 'Slippery Bob'—a dish of battered kangaroo brains fried in emu fat.*

Hobart Town Hall

57-63 Macquarie Street, Hobart

The Hobart Town Hall, built between 1864 and 1866, was designed by important Hobart architect Henry Hunter in Italianate Renaissance style, with grand Tuscan columns and a deep portico. Built at a cost of £20,000 on completion, it contributed to a legacy of debt due to lavish spending on public buildings at that time. The Town Hall was constructed in the very location where Lieutenant Governor David Collins erected his tent upon arrival in February 1804 (soon after, his modest house was also built in the nearby area). The grand staircase leading to the elaborate ballroom is crafted in cedar and Huon pine and well worth a visit. Hobart was declared a city in 1842 and, following an Act of Parliament, the Hobart Municipality in 1852. The Town Hall celebrated its 150th anniversary in 2016.

Mercantile Mutual Building

119 Macquarie Street, Hobart

This late Victorian office building combines classic Gothic and Edwardian styles in finely dressed stone. On the fourth storey stand marble Corinthian columns capped by a Gothic parapet with a circular roof and curved glazing. This eclectic insurance building is unique as there were few investing in Hobart at this time. When completed in 1908 the Mercantile Mutual building was the tallest in Hobart and the first to have a lift, taking patrons to the 'Cafe National' for afternoon tea on the rooftop terrace, a popular family outing. The Mercantile was designed by Alan Walker, who was also responsible for the Hobart GPO (EZ *four*) and the Carnegie Building (ARG *one*).

MAC NINE **Public Buildings and Supreme Court** | 21 Murray Street, Hobart

The public buildings facing Franklin Square were built between 1884 and 1887, and a third storey was added in the twentieth century. The Supreme Court was designed by architect William Porden Kay and built between 1860 and 1910. Constructed by the prolific local building firm Seabrook, these Classical Revival-style buildings are very impactful, not only in their quality, but also in their dominating form in the street. The Supreme Court, no longer in use for its intended purpose, sits idle, while the surrounding public buildings are all utilised by the state Treasury Department.

MAC TEN

Legal Offices | *131 Macquarie Street, Hobart*

This series of stone three-story commercial buildings proceed in a sedate but stylish fashion up Macquarie Street, the elegant office on the corner of an important intersection in the town has housed a legal office since its construction in 1838, due to its proximity to the public buildings and courtroom nearby. Circle on first floor denotes where J.W. Newland's famous Hobart streetscape was taken *(see page 12).*

Tasmanian Club | *132 Macquarie Street, Hobart*

Originally the Derwent Bank, founded in 1828 in opposition to the established Bank of Van Diemens Land, this Classical Revival-style building, built in 1846, had an additional front elevation designed by pardoned convict James Thomson. His Roman Doric columns provide a strong feature, as do the window shutters fitted in the bank manager's office to protect it from robbery under arms by bushrangers. The Tasmanian Club, developed for the regular association of prominent men in the society of that time, follows the pattern of early London clubs. The club has had the old bank building as its home since 1878; previously it gathered at the nearby hotel owned by Mr John Webb – now Hadley's Orient Hotel (MU *five*).

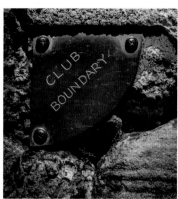

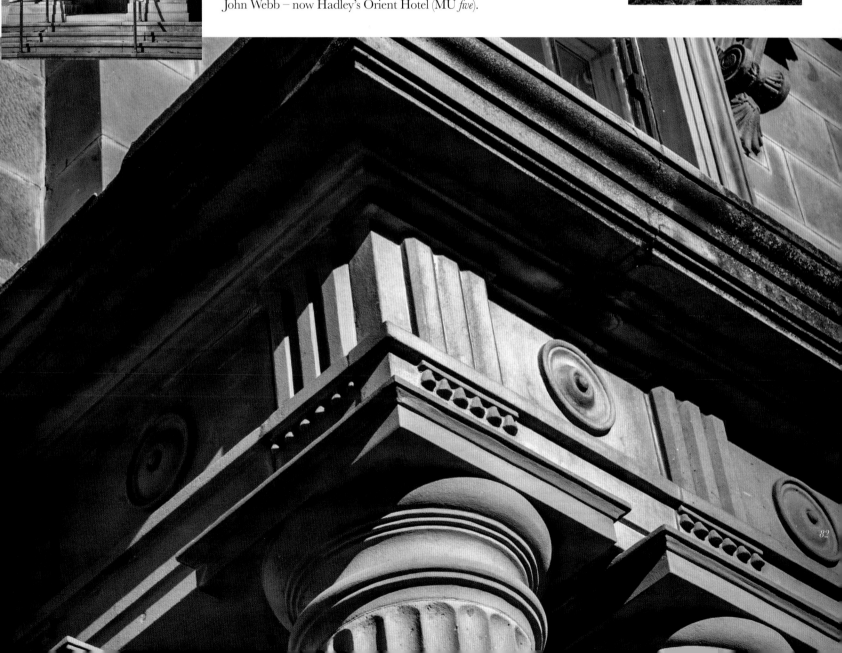

The Queen Mary Club | *143 Macquarie Street, Hobart*

Accomplished architect James Blackburn designed this stunning Bank of Australasia building in 1843, now in operation as the Queen Mary Club. The name 'Queen Mary Club' was granted by royal charter. Beginning in 1910 as a residential social club for Hobart women, the building was purchased from Mr Hadley (of Hadley's Orient Hotel – MU *five*) for £3,500. Set behind iron railings with stone piers, this symmetrical building is unique for not having a central entrance. It sits in the midst of an historic precinct, surrounded by early stone buildings.

Did You Know?

Van Diemens Land was named after Anthony Van Diemen, Governor-General of the Dutch East Indies. In 1642 Van Diemen sent Abel Janszoon Tasman in search of the great South Land. When Tasman arrived, he named it Van Diemens Land in honour of his patron. It is ironic and very Tasmanian that the people of Tasmania renamed it in honour of the subordinate Abel Tasman.

 **MAC THIRTEEN** ## St Joseph's Church | *165 Macquarie Street, Hobart*

This Gothic Revival Catholic church is built from locally quarried sandstone on land purchased by Father John Therry, who was sent to Van Diemens Land in 1838. A long legal battle delayed the construction of the cathedral in Harrington Street (HA *two*) so this smaller church was built first. Ex-convict architect James Thomson designed St Joseph's, with a dominant three-storey tower and castellated parapet. Several of the windows in the church are of international interest, as they were designed by Augustus Pugin. Bishop Wilson was a friend of Pugin, who contributed to several designs for Catholic buildings in Van Diemens Land in the 1840s.

 **MAC FOURTEEN**

The Hutchins School | *183 Macquarie Street, Hobart*

This school complex draws great inspiration from the Oxford and Cambridge campuses in England. This was the first work of architect William Archer. Here he delivers a Gothic Revival building, situated in grounds originally over two acres, in a prime central location in Macquarie Street. The school opened in 1849 at a cost of £2,367. The later use of these buildings was to house the Masonic Club of Tasmania.

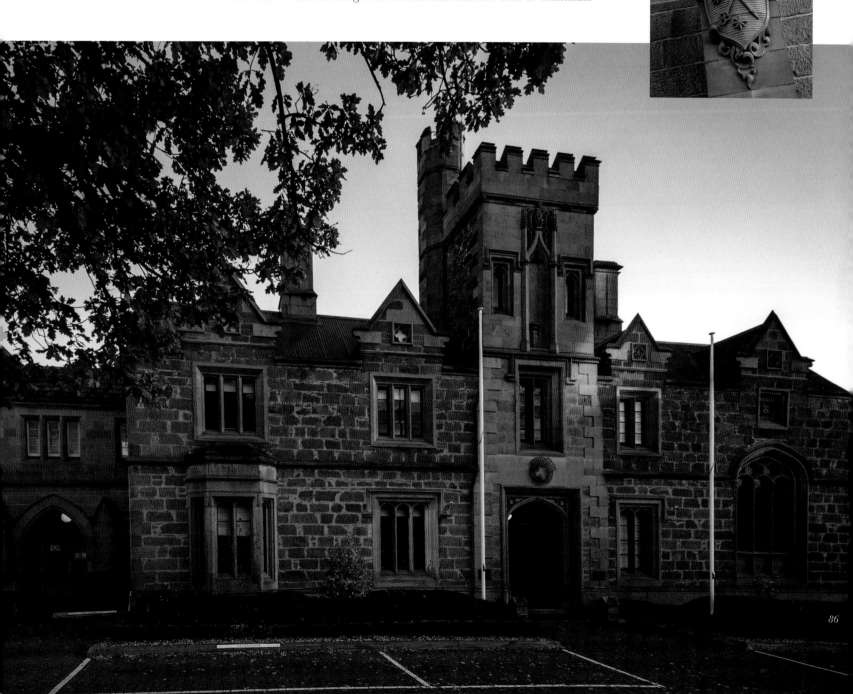

Macquarie Street - Architectural Features

EST 1836
WALCH

CORNWALL
INSURANCE
COMPANY.

Mr TOBYs
OFFICE
Up Stairs

341

SOUTH HOBART

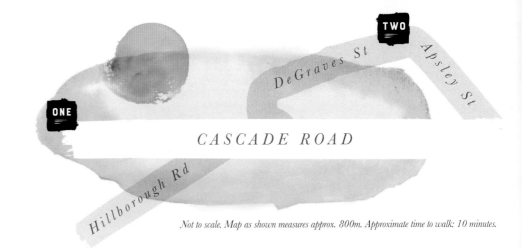

ONE · TWO

DeGraves St

Apsley St

CASCADE ROAD

Hillborough Rd

Not to scale. Map as shown measures approx. 800m. Approximate time to walk: 10 minutes.

The Hobart Rivulet passes through the suburb of South Hobart, nestled in the foothills of Mount Wellington. The heart of this community for the past 185 years has been the Cascade Brewery, an important landmark and point of reference. Due to its location, South Hobart's climate and weather patterns are often dictated by what is happening on the mountain. During the 19th century, South Hobart had the unusual distinction of being home to all three classes of citizens at that time, all within only four streets. There was a gated community for the lawmakers and wealthy members of society on what is now Davey Street; the middle class was situated on Cascade Road and upper Macquarie Street; and the lower socioeconomic area was adjacent to the rivulet, which was also home to the tannery, distillery, brewery and mill. At one stage, South Hobart possessed the more accurate and imaginative name 'Wellington Hamlets'.

SOHO ONE

Cascade Brewery
131 Cascade Road, South Hobart

On this site in 1824 was the first business venture by Peter DeGraves – a timber mill that operated for several years. DeGraves formulated a new direction in business that used the mountain-fresh water as an ingredient for brewing rather than a source of power for his milling enterprises. The building's development has been continual, and looks rather like a Victorian wedding cake. Its location at the foothills of Mount Wellington enabled easy access to Hobart Rivulet's water supply. The brewery's production was suspended, however, in 1967 when it came close to being completely destroyed by the horrific bushfires engulfing much of the state – only the structural walls were left standing – but incredibly the brewery was up and running again in just twelve weeks.

SOHO TWO | **Female Factory** | *16 DeGraves Street, South Hobart*

Nicknamed the 'Shadow of Death Valley', this cold and damp complex rarely saw the sun's rays, but often felt the might of the flooding rivulet, making life for the several hundred women and infant residents extremely uncomfortable. Yard One is the best preserved section of the Female Factory, but is just one of five yards that ran the entire length of DeGraves Street – all with high sandstone walls. Opening in 1828, the factory served the purpose of separating the female convict population from the men, and keeping the women busy with laborious tasks. During the 50 years of convict transportation, 13,000 female convicts arrived in Van Diemens Land. The factory finally closed in 1877, and today this site is the most significant in the country for the thousands of descendants of these women. The Female Factory is classified as a World Heritage site.

DAVEY St

FOUR
THREE
TWO
Brooker Hwy
SEVEN
ONE
NINE

DAVEY STREET

EIGHT
SIX **FIVE**

Darcy St
Southern Outlet
Molle St
Barrack St
Harrington St
Murray St
Elizabeth St
Argyle St
Campbell St

Not to scale. Map as shown measures approx. 2.6km. Approximate time to walk: 40 minutes.

MT. WELLINGTON FROM DOCK, HOBART.

Davey Street took its original name, Pitt Street, from the British Prime Minister in office at the end of the 18th century. Its name was later changed to Davey Street after the early Governor of Van Diemens Land, Thomas Davey, 1814-1817. Davey's governorship was unproductive for the most part. In Sydney his conduct was seen as 'low buffoonery'; a man of ill manners, low morals and with an expensive drinking habit. Macquarie eventually had Davey removed from office, replacing him with Governor William Sorell (1817-1824). At his death in 1823, Davey left an estate of less than £20. Davey Street, however, certainly became a very important part of Hobart Town, providing access to facilities such as the public hospital, the town cemetery, the waterfront and the military barracks.

Did You Know?

Under the command of Captain R. Fitzroy, the HMS Beagle undertook a circumnavigation of the world. On the ship's stay in the port of Hobart in February 1836, a young Charles Darwin made numerous observations, both geological and biological. He wrote at the time of departure a letter to his sister stating: 'If I emigrate, choose this rather than society on a pleasanter footing…free of contamination of rich convicts…colony appeared well governed…streets at night more orderly than those of an English town…gardens delightfully resemble England… all on board like this place better than Sydney.'

![DV ONE] **Royal Engineer's Building** | *2 Davey Street, Hobart*

The Royal Engineers arrived in Hobart Town in 1835 with the directive that all military works, convict buildings, ordinance and military stores should come under the Offices of the Ordinance Department. At this location, an extensive collection of buildings and workshops were a centre of activity for convicts producing building materials. It is here that engineers designed bridges, prisons and convict buildings for locations such as Norfolk Island, Maria Island and Port Arthur. The need thus arose for an office space, and in 1846 this two-storey sandstone building in Gothic Revival-style housed those engineers; a beautifully symmetrical building seen from the top of Macquarie Street looking east. The Tasmanian Main Line Railway Company operated from this spot from 1876 until the Transport Commission was established in 1938. The building was recently renovated by public subscription, grants and engineering firms, and is now home to The Institute of Engineers Australia.

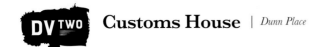

Customs House | *Dunn Place*

The original Customs House was designed by John Lee Archer and was opened in 1840, positioned at Salamanca Place near the New Wharf. Sharing this building with the Legislative Council and House of Assembly meant that towards the end of the nineteenth century additional space was required. The Tasmanian Government initiated the building of a new Customs House as part of Federation, which mean this project fell under Commonwealth responsibility. Orlando Baker was the architect under supervision. Engineers had many concerns to account for during the planning of the project, such as the huge depth of landfill the building sits atop (between 4 and 8 metres) as well as the abrasive sea salt and wind from the Tasman Sea. The statues on Customs House were carved by Hobart sculptor Charles Watson. An early version of the Australian coat of arms can be seen above the pediment on the building's facade. The new Customs House was a striking building viewed from the harbour, designed to obscure three sides of the Bond Store building (DV *three*). It gave Hobart a brand-new facade, as opposed to the colonial pile of bricks now behind it, which had taken pride of place for the previous 80 or so years. The elaborate Baroque Revival style aptly represents the country's new-found confidence, and is Tasmania's first Federation building.

DV THREE | **Bond Store** | *Dunn Place*

Designed by Colonial Architect David Lambe in approximately 1824, and built upon the black sand of Sullivans Cove beach, this four-level building was used to store bonded goods, including tea, tobacco and spirits. From the courtyard, accessible from the TMAG, you can see the water-powered hydraulic lift that was added in 1900 to service the store. When the Customs House was added at the turn of the century, the Bond Store's first level was relegated to a basement and was encroached upon by reclaimed earth reaching up to the ceiling. The building is completely obscured from view from the harbour. Thankfully this incredible Georgian store survives the modern thrust of Hobart in the twentieth century and is now a wonderful gallery space for the TMAG.

DV FOUR

Secretary's Cottage | *Dunn Place*

Situated on top of the embankment that graduated to the original shore of Sullivans Cove, this cottage dates to 1813 or perhaps earlier. It was originally built to accompany the Commissariat Store and then used as an office for the Government Lumber Yard. In 1828 architect John Lee Archer converted it into accommodation for the secretary to the then Governor, Sir George Arthur. This cottage is the last remaining building of the former Regal Reserve (demolished 1859). Today the cottage is part of the TMAG collection of buildings, offering an example of colonial furniture in a Georgian setting.

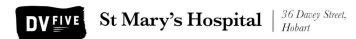

DV FIVE | St Mary's Hospital | *36 Davey Street, Hobart*

St Mary's Hospital, opened in 1847, is a Tudoresque building designed by well-regarded architect William Porden Kay. It was founded by Dr Bedford, a surgeon for the convict department who wanted to break away to start his own practice. He and a small group of medical practitioners made plans to begin a dispensary and hospital that the poor people of Hobart Town could afford. They also intended St Mary's to be a training hospital for doctors; however, the rather limited 60 beds didn't meet the Royal College of Surgeons' requirements. The hospital was designed to be self-supporting by means of public donations. One of its policies allowed any public subscriber to the hospital to nominate three outpatients a year, and poor people could now afford to buy hospital insurance for their families.

St David's Park | *Davey Street, Hobart*

St David's Park was Hobart Town's original burial ground. Selected by David Collins, the settlement's first governor, it would be where he was laid to rest in 1810, some six years after Hobart Town's founding. John Lee Archer later designed the memorial to Collins. The graveyard fell into an intolerable state of disrepair and, as all the cemeteries in Hobart Town were at that time being closed by the council, the resting places of the earliest of Hobart Town's settlers and pioneers were further disrespected during its conversion to St Davids Park in 1927. The lions at the entrance have been shoved from pillar to post, originally stationed at the entrance to the Bank of Van Diemens Land. After the bank's demolition,

the lions were relocated to Port Arthur. The bandstand is a central feature of the park and seen as one of the country's finest; its ceiling treated to preserve its acoustic properties.

Sacred
TO THE MEMORY OF
LACHLAN M. SORELL,
THE INFANT SON OF
L! GOVERNOR SORELL,
WHO DIED OCTOBER 20th 1822
AGED FOUR WEEKS AND FOUR DAYS

SLEEP ON FAIR FORM,
TH'ALMIGHTYS WILL BE DONE,
THEN RISE UNCHANGED,
AND BE AN ANGEL STILL

In memory of
T. HEATH
who was drowned
on the 15th of Sep.
1814
Aged 25 Years.

To the memory of
CAPTAIN JOHN LAUGHTON
Aged 33 Years
who was unfortunately Drowned off
Maria Island
1827
leaving behind him a Wife and 3 Children
to deplore his loss.
This Stone is erected by his Eldest Son
Mr Thomas Laughton
ALSO TO THE MEMORY OF
ELIZABETH wife of the above
who died Oct 11 1869 Aged 75 Years.

TO THE MEMORY OF
JOHN THOMSON
DIED
DEC 23RD 1833 AGED 33
YEARS

IN MEMORY OF
GEORGE WAL
January 1859
Aged 52 Years

TO THE MEMORY OF
SARAH ANN
the beloved wife of
JOHN SIDNEY BARHAM
who departed this life
Oct 21st 1857
Aged 36

HANNAH REDFERN
who died FEBRUARY 1863
AGED 2 YEARS

SARAH SCOFIELD
who died SEPT 1st 1860
AGED 48 YEARS

HANNAH REDFERN
who died
APRIL 11th 1868
AGED 7 YEARS

HERE RESTETH
the Body of
CHARLES HAYWOOD SEFTON
who Departed this life 1st September
ANNO DOMINI 1841
Aged 57 Years
ALSO
Ann Wife of CHARLES HAYWOOD SEFTON
who Died on the 8th December 1831
Aged 51 Years
Also
ELIZABETH BURGESS
who Died 11th April 1833
Aged 3 Weeks
Also ELIZABETH ROBERTS
Died 16th June 1875 Aged 3 Months

All images: St David's Park

BROW
25 December

MARIN
15 Feb 18 Aged 3 Month

AGNES
Nov 1832 Aged 1 Year

Sacred
TO THE MEMORY OF
DAVID COLLINS ESQ
LIEUTENANT GOVERNOR OF THIS COLONY
and Lt COLONEL of the ROYAL MARINE

JENNINGS LANE

1875
ROYAL TENNIS
COURT

TICKET OF LEAVE

Did You Know?

Charles Dickens' character 'Fagan' was based on a real person – the skilled pickpocket of London, Ikey Solomon. He arrived in Van Diemens Land determined to join his family, who had been transported. Despite arriving under an alias, he was arrested and shipped back to London and sentenced to 14 years in, you guessed it, Van Diemens Land, only to be given a ticket-of-leave four years later in 1835. Thereafter he established a tobacco shop on Elizabeth Street. He died a pauper.

The Royal Tennis Club

45 Davey Street,
Hobart

Royal Tennis was introduced to Tasmania by Samuel Smith Travers in 1874-75. The design is based on the courts in London and it's the earliest court in Australia. The club at present has a local membership of over 200 players, including the current and longstanding World Men's Singles Champion, Rob Fahey (at the time of printing). The clubrooms were extended to include an earlier brewery warehouse building on Davey Street, dating from 1831.

Anglesea Barracks

96-120 Davey Street, Hobart

In 1811 the Governor of New South Wales, Lachlan Macquarie, made his first inspection of Hobart Town, following the sudden death of Van Diemens Land's first governor, David Collins. Macquarie deemed the facilities for the 73rd regiment as inappropriate. On December 2nd 1811 Macquarie rode to the top of the hill and examined the proposed location for the barracks, overlooking the camp and Sullivans Cove below. This would remain the headquarters for the Redcoats until their recall in 1870. The barracks, the oldest still in operation in the country, were given their official name 'Anglesea' by Governor Sir George Arthur after the Marquis of Hastings.

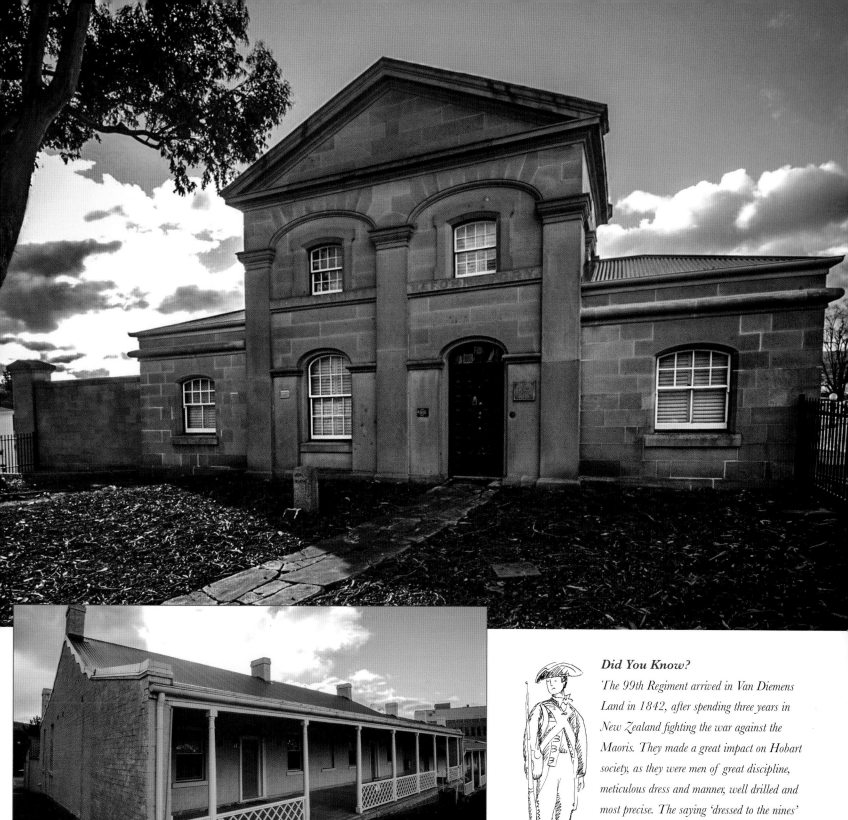

Did You Know?

The 99th Regiment arrived in Van Diemens Land in 1842, after spending three years in New Zealand fighting the war against the Maoris. They made a great impact on Hobart society, as they were men of great discipline, meticulous dress and manner, well drilled and most precise. The saying 'dressed to the nines' comes from the perfection of the Redcoats' personal attire and grooming. At the Anglesea Barracks is a monument to those men, the only monument to a foreign regiment in the country.

NAVY
HEADQUARTERS
TASMANIA

107

Field Officers' Quarters

Anglesea Army Barracks c1814

The dramatic entrance of this former private residence is one of Hobart's finest; its portico of majestic Huon pine is, however, recycled from the demolition of a Macquarie Street house. Islington, built in 1847, is in the true Regency style. Today, it is a highly regarded boutique hotel and one of Tasmania's most awarded accommodation providers.

Davey Street - Architectural Features

110

COLLINS ST

Not to scale. Map as shown measures approx. 600m. Approximate time to walk: 7 minutes.

COLLINS STREET, HOBART.

Collins Street was named after Lieutenant Governor David Collins 1756 -1810. His vast experience in Australian affairs, having been a member of the first fleet expedition to Botany Bay, led to him being chosen to form a new settlement at Port Phillip on the south coast of what is now Victoria. With the failure of that location, Collins moved his attention and settlement to Sullivans Cove on the River Derwent. Very few remnants of the Georgian period exist in Collins Street, even though it was one of the initial seven streets. It is marked by the rivulet at its beginning near Molle Street and the rivulet's end near Campbell Street. Also named after David Collins is St Davids Park (DV *six*) and St Davids Cathedral (MU *four*).

111

Stonehenge Cottage

225 Collins Street, Hobart

This is Hobart's earliest surviving timber building. Constructed from hand-sawn timbers, it has a shallow sandstone rubble foundation, iron-hipped roof, original 12-paned windows and round-headed fanlight above the central doorway. This is a marvel of survival considering its close proximity to the CBD and its 20th century industrial surrounds. Referred to by some as 'Hobart's Stonehenge', this little cottage is thought to be dated around 1825.

Walker's Brewery and Flour Mill

210 Collins Street, Hobart

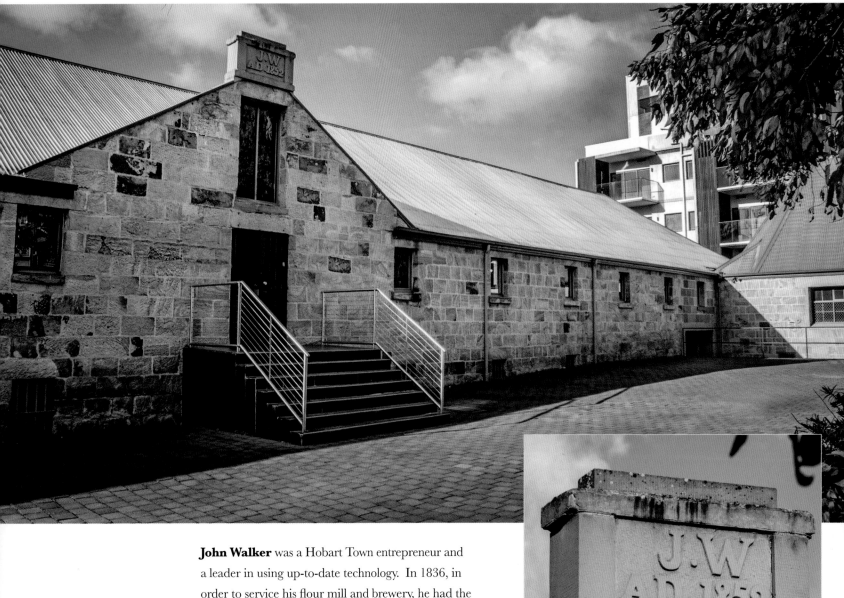

John Walker was a Hobart Town entrepreneur and a leader in using up-to-date technology. In 1836, in order to service his flour mill and brewery, he had the first steam engine built to replace the irregular flow of the previously used Hobart Rivulet. This present mill, built by Walker in 1852, had a gross turnover of 25,000 pounds of flour in its first year of production, and in 1854 peaked in sales at £68,000. The Malt House to the right was purchased by the Cascade Brewery (SoHo *one*) in 1883. To this day the rivulet runs behind the rear wall of this inner-city brewery and mill building.

Original Malt House ceiling

Cascade Brewery Office

154 Collins Street, Hobart

This building was the Cascade Brewery Company's administration building for well over a century until newly designed facilities were added recently at the brewery site. This Victorian Free Classical-style, two-storey building has a very decorative parapet, featuring a beer barrel and thylacine sculpture on top.

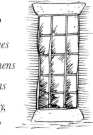

Did You Know?

When Peter DeGraves arrived in Van Diemens Land in 1824 it was with his entire family, on his own ship and with equipment on board to begin a new life. He established a sawmill but, soon after, unexpected events began to unfold. A debt had followed him all the way from London and he was committed to the dilapidated Old Hobart Town Gaol in May 1826, where he served five years in the debtors' section.

115

T&G Building

| *113-117 Collins Street,*
| *Hobart*

One of Hobart's finest examples of Art Deco architecture, built in 1938 during the temperance and general mutual life society of Australia's expansion throughout the country. The Architects were A&K Henderson. The T&G Building is listed as a notable Tasmanian building of the 20th Century by the Royal Australian Institute of Architects.

Did You Know?

Thomas Davey was appointed Lieutenant-Governor of Van Diemens Land in 1812. Lachlan Macquarie, Governor of New South Wales, described Davey as a drunk who showed 'an incredible degree of frivolity and buffoonery in his manners'.

On royal birthdays, Tom Davey gave out free rum, dispensing it from a keg in front of the governor's house. He also invented a cocktail, named 'Blow My Skull'. It was made by dissolving 165g (¾ cup) of brown cane sugar into a litre of water, then adding the juice of six limes (about 180ml), 500ml each of porter and navy-style rum (57% alcohol content) and 250ml of strong brandy. Davey built a lean-to on the Domain where he invited guests to a drinking session consuming the potent Blow My Skull brew, and then they staggered back into Hobart Town.

Hobart Rivulet

The Hobart Rivulet's source is from the majestic Mount Wellington, and throughout Hobart's history it has had a vital role in the town's development. It has a character of its own. While being at heart the reason for Hobart Town's settlement location on the western side of the River Derwent, it has also provided its citizens for the first twenty years with mountain-fresh water and turned every water wheel of industry along the way. However, its character could turn villainous, destroying bridges, inundating businesses with water, flooding basements and spreading water-borne disease throughout the community. The rivulet today is somewhat contained by a subterranean tunnel, carrying the rivulet's flow under the city, beneath plazas, car parks, streets and the hospital, before entering the River Derwent in a new course, diverting the original stream away from the port and harbour activity, towards the Cenotaph and regatta grounds east of the city.

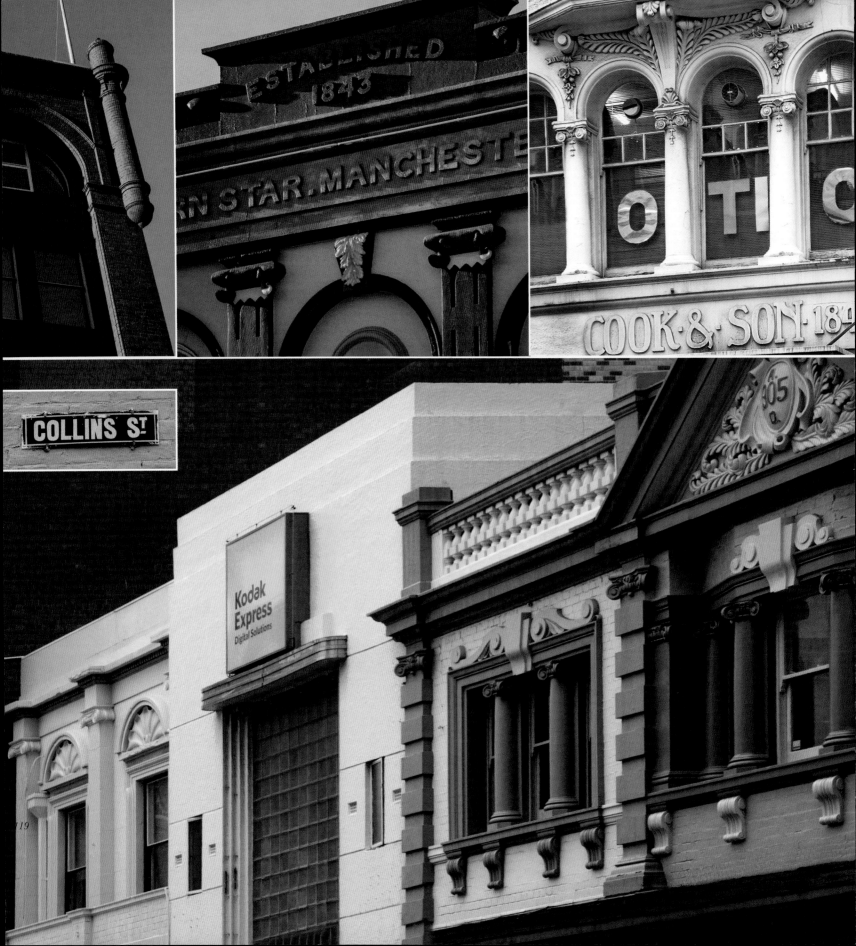

ESTABLISHED
1843

RN STAR. MANCHESTE

OTIC

COOK & SON 18

COLLINS St

Kodak
Express
Digital Solutions

119

Warwick Street - Architectural Features

WARWICK ST

This street of dips and steep rises was named after the Earl of Warwick, George William Evans, who emigrated to NSW in 1802 and worked as a surveyor and explorer. He became Deputy Surveyor of the Lands Department in Van Diemens Land, resigning in 1825 due to a corruption challenge. Evans then lived in England until 1844, but returned to Hobart Town to spend his final days, passing away here in 1852.

WARRICK STREET

ONE

Elizabeth St

Church St

Church St

Argyle St

Map: Archives Office of Tasmania

WK ONE | **Holy Trinity Church** | *50 Warwick Street, Hobart*

The Holy Trinity Church stands on an elevated site in North Hobart at the intersection of Church and Warwick streets. John Lee Archer chose this location, though famed ex-convict architect James Blackburn executed the church's design. There may not be a more commanding place of worship in Hobart, though St Georges Church (BP *one*) in Battery Point also occupies a position of great advantage. The foundation stone was laid by then-governor Sir John Franklin in 1841, but due to lack of funds the church could not be completed until consecrated in 1849. One of Blackburn's finest works of this scale, its Gothic style is quite striking. It features a massive four-level entry tower and contains one of the country's oldest set of bells.

122

Map: Archives Office of Tasmania
Map - Sprents Page 60 - Bounded by Warwick, Argyle, Patrick
& Church Streets, Paternoster Row intersecting Warwick &
Patrick Sts (Sec H2) Hobart AF393-1-58

MELVILLE ST

Viscount Melville 1771-1851 hailed from Scotland. When he entered politics, he was assigned the task of maintaining the British Navy's fleet. Melville resigned in 1830 and died in 1851.

Did You Know?

The infamous bushranger Martin Cash, 1808-77, while on the run with his gang Cash & Co., was drawn into Hobart Town by the passion of revenge. Cash's mistress Bessie Clifford was said to be seeing another, so Cash disguised himself as a sailor and came to take his revenge in the form of a cold-blooded double murder on the 29th August 1843. Cash, however, was recognised, and a chase through Hobart Town's streets unfolded. At the Old Commodore Inn (now Brisbane Hotel) he ran into an off-duty police officer and fired his weapon, shooting off the fingers of one man and disfiguring another with a bullet to the face. Thus, Cash was due to hang for his many misdemeanours. His sentence, however, was changed to life imprisonment at the last minute.

THE FOUNDATION STONE OF THIS CHURCH WAS LAID ON DECEMBER 27TH 1837. BY SIR JOHN FRANKLIN. THE ARCTIC EXPLORER. THEN GOVERNOR OF THIS ISLAND

MEL ONE **Methodist Church Buildings** | *56-58 Melville Street, Hobart*

These buildings have significance due to the early formation of the Methodists in Van Diemens Land. As early as 1822 a nascent group of Wesleyans advertised in the *Hobart Town Gazette* asking for a donation of 100,000 bricks for the construction of a chapel, and in 1837 Sir John Franklin, the then governor, laid the first stone. Benjamin Nokes was the leader of the early Methodist Church in Hobart Town, meeting with his congregation in a private house in Collins Street. Nokes recorded that the locals were so opposed to the unfamiliar sound of praises being sung that they voiced their disapproval in terms of stones, bricks, serpents and dead dogs. The recessed two story Georgian building has a symmetrical three-bayed stuccoed facade, and a simple portico with Ionic columns.

ONE

MELVILLE STREET

Elizabeth St

Murray St

Douglas Armati at his home Stanwell Hall c1826, Melville Street,
West Hobart. Holding original painting by celebrated colonial painter,
John Glover who also lived at this residence.

125

Melville Street - Architectural Features

126

BATHURST ST

1889

CAMPBELL & MINCHIN CHAMBERS.

Bathurst Street - Architectural Features

128

LIVERPOOL ST

Lord Liverpool, 1770–1828, was elected to the House of Commons in 1790 at 20 years of age and served as Secretary of State for War and the Colonies. He became Prime Minister in 1812 and remained so for 15 years. The street was named by Macquarie in 1811, after this obviously very influential person in the British Empire.

LIVERPOOL STREET

TWO

ONE

THREE

Elizabeth St

Argyle St

Campbell St

Brooker Hwy

Not to scale. Map as shown measures approx. 450m. Approximate time to walk: 6 minutes.

Liverpool Street, Hobart, Tasmania 1910.

129

 Railway Roundabout | *Brooker Highway, Hobart*

The Railway Roundabout, located at the intersection of the Brooker Highway and Liverpool Street, was built to enable passengers from the railway terminus nearby to access the city via its two pedestrian subways. Built in 1963 in an innovative Modernistic Sputnik style, the central fountain continues to obtain accolades and awards, even as recently as 2015, when the Roundabout Appreciation Society awarded it their prestigious 'One-Way Gyratory Accolade'. The fountain still uses the original hydraulic and electrical system installed over half a century ago. A national competition to design Hobart's roundabout was run in 1960 and won by a group of three including Vere Cooper, engineer Rod Cuthbert and local artist Geoff Parr. A popular feature of their design was a backlighting effect achieved using colourful beams of light on the fountain spray at night.

LV TWO | **Menzies Research Institute** | *17 Liverpool Street, Hobart*

The Menzies Research Institute has developed significantly since its modest beginning in the 1980s, when the University of Tasmania established the Menzies Centre for Population Health Research. Evolving into the Menzies Research Institute in 2004, it has gained a reputation for its work in epidemiology and groundbreaking discoveries in the area of SIDS. The Menzies complex took eight years to build, but has achieved an energy-efficiency green rating of 5, the second highest rating a building can achieve. Inside the Medical Science building is a louvre system to control sunlight. The Research Building, designed by Melbourne architectural firm Lyon, has a concrete façade, flowing arches and slanted windows. The architects' intention was to use the steel-framed fenestration as an abstract expression of the surrounding mountains, Derwent River and other contours of topography.

National Australia Bank | *76 Liverpool Street, Hobart*

In 1922, during a period of rapid industrial expansion and economic growth, the Melbourne-based National Australia Bank directed its interest to Hobart. They purchased the site where the bank stands today for an unprecedented £32,000.

Liverpool Street - Architectural Features

QUEENS DOMAIN

Queens Domain was given to the people of Hobart in 1860, although it was already accommodating military facilities, a Government House under construction and the well-established Botanical Gardens. The land's original occupiers left plenty of evidence of their habitation, for there are middens located there to this day. A large portion of the domain remains grassland and wooded areas, protecting an array of indigenous birdlife. Today the Queens Domain, unfortunately at one stage called 'The Queen's Paddock', is home to the Royal Hobart Regatta Grounds, the Hobart Cenotaph, the Soldier's Memorial Walk, the TCA Ground (former home of Tasmanian cricket), the Hobart Aquatic Centre, the Hobart International Tennis Centre, Domain House and the University of Tasmania buildings, the hilly suburb of Glebe, the Domain Athletic Centre and is the site of the former Beaumaris Zoo (1923-1937).

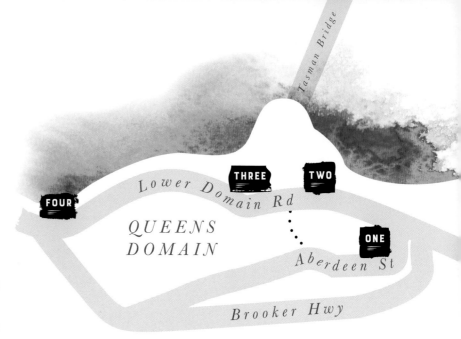

Not to scale. Map as shown measures approx. 3km. Approximate time to walk: 40 minutes.

 Domain House | *Aberdeen Street, Hobart*

The High School of Hobart Town was built from a design by Alexander Dawson and was an extremely important mark in the development of education in Van Diemens Land. The school was opened in 1850 and later used as Christ College, then as the original University of Tasmania, who occupied the building until 1980. UTAS moved to modern buildings at a main campus in Sandy Bay during the 1960s. The Domain House School Building is an idiosyncratic type of Gothic design; three storeys high, with a grand staircase lit by a tall perpendicular window. The front features smoothly finished sandstone, whereas the rear and sides are of rubble, due to a somewhat limited budget.

Government House
Hobart

QUEENS DOMA

Scale—Four chains to one inch

See FIELD BOOK No. 936
P. N. 32

136

Map - Hobart 94 - Plan of Queens Domain, Hobart -
surveyor Hall (Field Book 936) Archives Office of Tasmania

Government House | *7 Lower Domain Road, Hobart*

James Blackburn, the ex-convict architect, was appointed in 1837 to design Government House. Though work began in 1842, there was a problem because the authorities in London had not granted permission to build. As a result of being left out of the process, they ordered the building, now at foundation stage, to be demolished. The then-governor of Van Diemens Land was not able to obtain a permit or the means to build until 1858, when William Porden Kay, taking the place of Blackburn, designed what is considered the most comfortable governor's residence in all of the colonies, at a cost of £67,000. This Gothic Baronial Revival building is picturesquely set on a hill among grassland on which cattle graze. The 10-hectare estate

has numerous stone buildings. Only the very finest materials and furnishings were employed. The building was constructed from brown sandstone quarried from the Queens Domain. White stone to finish the building was also found in the grounds; that quarry site is now the magnificent Government House pond. Set into the face of the large square tower to the north is a grand clock. Porden Kay personally selected many of the fittings and furnishings for the building while visiting London during construction. Most notable is the main ballroom, which has a high vaulted ceiling and huge chandeliers. This building stands today as an example to the world of the very best of 19th century Australian architecture.

Images by Paul County - Courtesy Government House Tasmania

138

140

Images by Paul County - Courtesy Government House Tasmania

QD THREE Botanical Gardens | *Lower Domain Road, Hobart*

Established during the governorship of William Sorell in 1818, the gardens, though open to the public, had limited access and no set design. By 1835 the gardens were starting to be landscaped and properly planned and in 1843 became the interest of the Royal Society of Tasmania. The Royal Tasmanian Botanical Gardens, as they are now known, are the second oldest in Australia. The impressive iron entrance gates, an iconic feature, were commissioned in 1877. Of international interest are the convict-built walls. These not only enclose the gardens, but also installed within the walls are fireplaces with lengthy flues and air-ducts, distributing warmth so that plants used to a warmer climate can grow nearby.

Cornelian Bay Boat Houses

Queens Walk,
Cornelian Bay, Hobart

Land owners in the Cornelian Bay area had the great advantage of water frontage, and made full use of this by having their own jetties and boat sheds, the first appearing as early as 1892. By 1913 there were six boat sheds, all of which had to by law be licensed. They were built to a specific plan set out by the Marine Board. Between 1922 and 1978, the Hobart City Council took over administration for the boat shed licences. Many of the sheds remained in family ownership for decades.

143

WATERFRONT

HUNTER STREET

(Old Wharf)

ONE

Davey St

Parliament House, Hobart.

SEVEN

SIX

Runnymede St

FIVE

CASTRAY ESPLANADE

(New Wharf)

SALAMANCA PLACE

Morrison St

FOUR

THREE

Montpelier Retreat

TWO

145

Black & white images: Tasmanian Archives and Heritage Office

Hunter Street was formerly known as Old Wharf, preceded by Hunter Island, where the settlement's very first construction was undertaken in February 1804: a timber jetty to receive stores and people. This small island in Sullivans Cove enabled access at a low tide via a sand bar. Due to the exceptionally deep anchorage on this side of the harbour, merchants and entrepreneurs built the first warehouses here in order to capitalise on Hobart Town's growing maritime industry, which centred on whaling and shipbuilding. This is also where tens of thousands of convict men and women disembarked upon arrival from Great Britain. By the 1800s the industry focus at Old Wharf was shifting to jam production and fruit canning, and for the next 100 years G. Peacock & Sons, and then H. Jones & Co. established an enormous trade with numerous countries, utilising their own fleet of ships. This would contribute to rebranding Tasmania 'The Apple Isle'. Hobart's IXL Jam Factory, just one of the branches of the IXL company operating all around the world, was the largest in the Southern Hemisphere, and included every building you see today on Hunter Street. After the sale of H. Jones & Co. the State Government purchased the IXL complex. Some buildings sat idle for twenty years before the precinct had new life injected into it as a hub for culture and the arts, including the award-winning Henry Jones Art Hotel, which absorbed most of the historic Old Wharf Georgian buildings.

147

Henry Jones Art Hotel interior

Parliament House

This building originally served as the Customs House and was designed by John Lee Archer in 1835. Inspired by the recently completed customs building in London, he adopted some of its features to create an enduring structure of strength and dignity – a two-storey Classic Revival. Its basement is fully intact, with convict brick vaults marked with the broad arrow. In 1841 the Legislative Council moved in and shared this building with the customs offices, which were relocated in 1901. In 1856 the first House of Assembly met and, to this day, Archer's stunning design is home to both. Houses of Parliament.

Parliament House interior

149

WF THREE Salamanca Place

The Old Wharf at Hunter Street had served Hobart Town for thirty years, but now industry was overtaking the Old Wharf's capabilities, so in 1831 convicts were put to work quarrying dolerite rock to construct a 'New Wharf'. Previously, work of a similar nature done on the other side of the cove had the benefit of available sandstone. The situation at New Wharf was not so fortunate, with access to only the much harder dolerite stone. Convicts working on the quarrying were stationed on the prison ship *Success* moored in the cove. In 1834 the New Wharf was officially opened, but the construction of sandstone warehouses occurred later, between 1835 and 1860.

Salamanca Market

Salamanca Place - market every Saturday between 8.30am and 3.00pm

Georgian-styled sandstone warehouses in the foreground, Salamanca Place lined with market stalls and a snow-capped mountain in the background is one of the iconic images of Hobart.

The warehouses were built by convict stonemasons in the mid 1800s and they plied their trade for close to 100 years, but by the 1970s most were vacant, derelict and facing demolition.

The Hobart Council decided an open-air market would revitalise the area and held the first in 1972 with a handful of stalls:

the novelty of an event on a Saturday was enough to attract a crowd of 15,000.

One year later, the state government bought some of the warehouses to set up an arts centre and, combined with the market, it was the start of the area's renaissance.

Salamanca Market is now the longest-running market in the city's history and the state's number one tourist attraction. With over 300 stalls, you can meet the people who have produced or made the goods they are selling and discover anything from artisan jewellery and handcrafted timber to vintage collectables and delicious treats.

152

KELLY STREET
JANUARY 1840
J.K.

WF FIVE

Kellys Steps

5 Kelly Street/
Salamanca Place, Hobart

This historic thoroughfare is not only quaint and practical, but also has a link to one of the colony's great characters, Captain James Kelly. Born in Parramatta in 1791 to a poor family, Kelly would, as a young man, command his own ship, become the first Australian-born harbour master, own land and, famously, sail a five-oar whale boat for 49 days around Van Diemens Land in 1815-16. Kelly had a four-acre land grant in Battery Point and in 1839 had steps built to gain easier access up the steep cutting from Salamanca Place to Battery Point. These steps would become a convenient shortcut for mariners between the waterfront and their cottages. Kelly Street, connected to the steps, was named in 1840.

Did You Know?

Sir George Arthur's tenure as Governor when ended in 1836 after twelve years, was seen out with a very public departure, proceeding down Murray Street toward the vessel at New Wharf that would take him to his next post, in Upper Canada. The Street lined with Red Coates both sides of the Street in full military uniform, gave him the send off he so desired. The other send off he got that day he did not see coming, the send off from the free people, the majority of those were ex-convicts, and they gave Governor Arthur quiet the farewell, hurling obscenities, booing and hissing and launching objects as he passed by, and although Sir George was an esteemed gentleman of the Empire, he could be seen visibly by the entire audience sobbing uncontrollably.

 Ordinance Stores | *15-17 Castray Esplanade, Hobart*

The Ordinance Stores, giving an impression of solidity and strength, presented a commanding sight for vessels approaching the safe port of Hobart Town. These stone buildings – one three-storey, the other four-storey – were built to the design of John Lee Archer in 1834, who also envisaged a grander precinct, never built. Tunnels leading from the rear of the stores went to the top of the hill behind, the site of Mulgrave Battery, where large stone chambers securely stored gunpowder and military goods.

154

WF SEVEN | Signal Station | *19-21 Castray Esplanade, Hobart*

The earliest method of warning Hobart Town authorities of an approaching ship was a convict-manned lookout on Betsey Island, where smoke signals were used to raise the alarm when a vessel neared the entrance of the Derwent River. In 1811 Governor Macquarie ordered a semaphore station to be built on Mount Nelson, and then another on the Tasman Peninsula, both utilising a communication method of different flags. Messages dispatched from Port Arthur could be deciphered and spelled out in Hobart Town within fifteen minutes. These semaphores were up to ninety feet high, with arms to be raised and lowered – an elaborate system stretching across southeast Van Diemens Land. The semaphore system was later overtaken by the telephone.

Situated above the Salamanca Place precinct and overlooking the Derwent River and Mount Wellington, Battery Point is a very desirable location. The first residence on Battery Point was 'Cottage Green', the home and garden, amounting to 50 acres, of the colony's first reverend, Robert Knopwood. Mulgrave Battery was added to help protect Hobart Town from possible attack by the French navy; the semaphore station was instituted to improve communication, otherwise development was slow. Subdivision of the area occurred in the 1830s along with the New Wharf development, which is now Salamanca Place. Battery Point became a hive of shipbuilding, and many fine ships were constructed on the foreshore from outstanding local timbers.

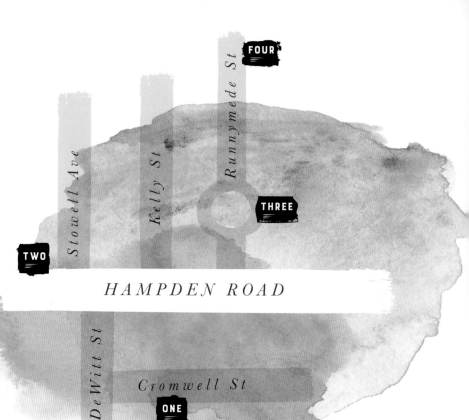

FOUR

Runnymede St

Stowell Ave

Kelly St

THREE

TWO

HAMPDEN ROAD

DeWitt St

Cromwell St

ONE

BATTERY POINT

157

Tasmanian Archives and Heritage Office - Arthur Circus 1930s

St Georges Church

30 Cromwell Street,
Battery Point

An imposing double act once stood on Battery Point hill – close to St Georges Church was a grand windmill of equal height, causing quite an impact to the skyline as viewed from the harbour and town. Sadly, the windmill was demolished long ago. Two of Van Diemens Land's most highly regarded architects contributed to St Georges – John Lee Archer designed the nave and James Blackburn the Romanesque tower. The formidable portico with large Doric columns was a later addition by a third architect, Robert Hudson. The church was consecrated in 1838, minus its tower and portico.

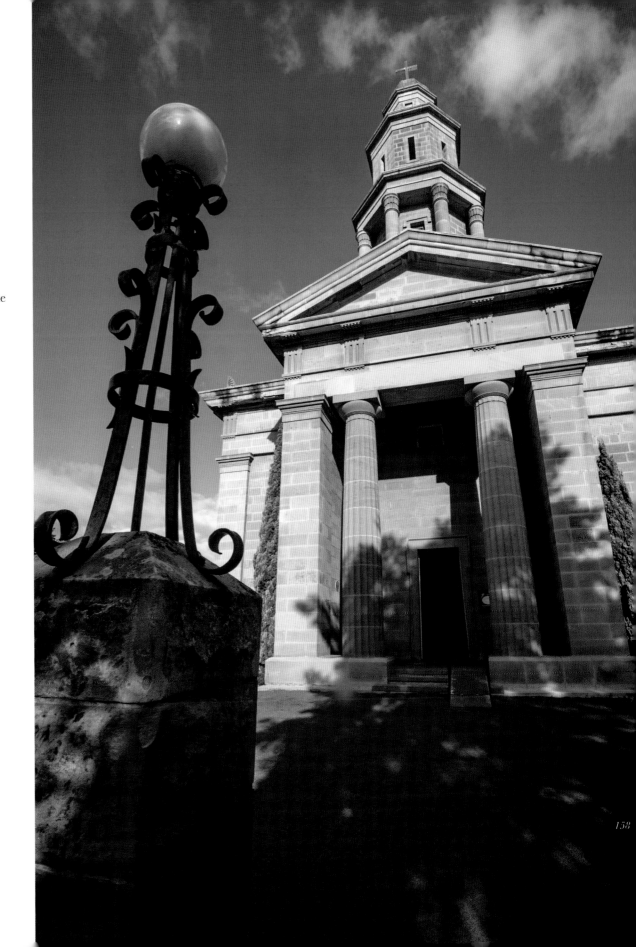

158

159   **An opportunity to visit** the Georgian house of a gentleman is quite a treat, and the happy relationship between Narryna and the public is one stretching over many decades. Although unashamedly simplistic externally, its dignified stonework, grand entrance and shallow fanlight are all appealing features. The high walls that enclose the property are impressive, to say the least, and the fountain and mature plants are a tranquil sight for visitors. Commissioned by Captain Haig, a wealthy merchant established in Hobart Town in the 1820s, it was completed in 1834. The architect was Edward Finch.

Arthur Circus

Arthur Circus is a throwback to another time – in a way, a relic of old-fashioned town planning. Forming a distinctive streetscape in a tight urban neighbourhood these sixteen brick and timber cottages are haphazardly arranged around a tiny central park, which was initially referred to as 'pleasure grounds' in an attempt to lure the prospective landowner. Lieutenant Governor Arthur himself designed this speculative development. The lots were purchased and occupied during the 1850s.

160

BP FOUR Lenna | 20 Runnymede Street, Battery Point

This Italianate home was designed for merchant and shipbuilder Alexander McGregor in the late 1870s. It was completed in several stages, and in photographs of early Hobart this striking building certainly stands out on the shoulder of Battery Point. McGregor was responsible for building the largest fleet of ships owned by an individual south of the Equator. These ships were regarded as superior due to the locally sourced and exceptionally hardy blue gums from which they were made. Lenna takes its name from the indigenous word for 'house' or 'hut'. It was purchased in 1971 by Innkeepers and has functioned as a hotel since.

Battery Point - Architectural Features

HAMPDEN ROAD

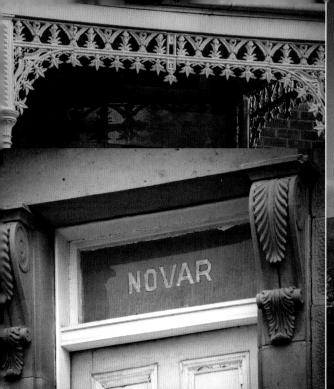

NOVAR

KELLY ST
HAMPDEN

ARTHUR CIRCUS

SLOANE S

CHELTENHAM PLACE

CHELTENHAM
PLACE

23

165

FINLAY ST

Battery Point - Architectural Features

166

Nanny Goat Lane

WREST POINT

WP ONE **Wrest Point** | *410 Sandy Bay Road, Sandy Bay*

The Federal Group is the longest continuously running hotel group in Australia, beginning with its purchase of the Federal Coffee Palace Company in Melbourne and later including the Savoy Plaza and famous Windsor Hotel, also in Melbourne. Moving its attention to Tasmania, the Federal Group purchased Wrest Point Riviera Hotel on Chaffeys Point, Sandy Bay, in 1956. The Riviera opened in 1939 and was not only stylish, known as the place to dance and be entertained, but its design, by architect Keith Wildman, is still considered an excellent example of Art Deco. In 1968, with the support of the government and a controversial referendum, the Federal Group was granted the first casino licence in Australia. In February 1973, the Sir Roy Grounds-designed octagonal casino tower, still Tasmania's tallest building at 73 metres, opened its doors, paving the way for further licences throughout the country.

ONE

Drysdale Ave

SANDY BAY ROAD

YOUDO HOBART HISTORY WALKS

YouDo Hobart History Walks explore the history of the Hobart city area, encompassing Hobart's oldest buildings, its industrial past and convict transportation. The walks include religious and free settler history, colonial governors and administrations, bushrangers, public executions and fascinating cultural stories. Beginning with the founding of Hobart Town in 1804, the walks explore Hobart's history from the Georgian period of the early 19th century through to the 20th century.

Walks depart at 1.30pm and 3.30pm daily unless otherwise stated.

Also available is the YouDo Hobart History app. The app is location-sensitive and downloadable from the iTunes App Store. The app includes colourful stories and images of Hobart's historic characters and built history. Timelines are included and there are audio files suitable for iPhones and tablets.

www.youdohobart.com
0439 346 838

(See advertorial pages)

HERBACEOUS TOURS

www.herbaceoustours.com.au
sally@herbaceoustours.com.au

0416 970 699 – Sally

(See advertorial pages)

THE TENCH - PENITENTIARY CHAPEL HISTORIC SITE

6 Brisbane Street, Hobart
www.nationaltrust.org.au/tas

03 6231 0911

(See advertorial pages)

CASCADE FEMALE FACTORY HISTORIC SITE

16 Degraves Street, South Hobart
www.femalefactory.org.au

1800 139 478

(See advertorial pages)

RUNNYMEDE HOUSE

61 Bay Road, New Town
www.nationaltrust.org.au/places/runnymede/

03 6278 1269

GOURMANIA FOOD TOURS

An award-winning Hobart food tour
www.gourmaniafoodtours.com.au

0419 180 113 - Mary

HOBART COMEDY TOURS

www.hobartcomedytours.com

NARRYNA HERITAGE MUSEUM

103 Hampden Road, Battery Point
www.tmag.tas.gov.au/visitor_information/house_museums/narryna_heritage_museum

03 6234 2791

RED DECKER COMPANY

Brooke Street Pier Hobart
www.reddecker.com.au

03 6236 9116

CASCADE BREWERY TOURS

140 Cascade Road, South Hobart
www.cascadebrewery.com.au

03 6244 1117

HOBART HISTORIC CRUISES

03 6200 9074

HERITAGE HORSE DRAWN CARRIAGES

Salamanca Place
www.hobarthorsetours.com.au

0408 763 392

PENNICOTT WILDERNESS JOURNEYS

Dock Head Building
Franklin Wharf, Hobart
www.pennicottjourneys.com.au

03 6234 4270

TASMANIAN SEAFOOD SEDUCTION

(Seafood experience river cruise)

03 6234 4270

PRIVATE SECRETARY'S COTTAGE TOUR

Tasmanian Museum and Art Gallery
Booking required
www.tmag.tas.gov.au

03 6165 7000

(TMAG offers a wide variety of special interest tours. Phone or check website for details.)

DERWENT RIVER CHARTER

www.hobartyachts.com.au
mark@hobartyachts.com.au

0438 399 477

LARK WHISKY TOURS

The Lark Distillery Tour
Take a look behind the scenes of the Lark Distillery and discover the process, ingredients and art that goes into creating our award winning single malt whisky.
3 hours approx.

The Premium Lark Experience
A more immersive experience, this tour offers a full day of learning, hands-on production and tastings at the Lark Distillery.

www.larkdistillery.com

03 6231 9088

DRINK TASMANIA TOURS

www.drinktasmania.com.au
bookings@drinktasmania.com.au

0475 000 120

HOBART SNAPSHOT TOURS

www.hobartsnapshottours.com.au

0407 968 887

UNDER DOWN UNDER TOURS

(Includes Mt Wellington Descent)

www.underdownunder.com.au

1800 444 442

TOURS TASMANIA

http://www.tourstas.com.au/

1800 777 103

GHOST TOURS OF HOBART

0467 687 004

HOBART WALKING TOURS

0413 383 207

www.hobartwalkingtours.com.au

EXPERIENCE TASMANIA BUS TOURS

129 Liverpool Street Hobart
www.experiencetas.com.au

03 6234 3560

HOBART SHUTTLEBUS COMPANY

www.hobartshuttlebus.com

0408 341 804

HOBART HISTORIC TOURS

www.hobarthistorictours.com.au

03 6234 5550

HOBART'S TRIKEMANIA ADVENTURE TOURS

Murray Street Pier

0408 655 923

SETTLEMENT SECRETS

www.antipodeanentertainment.com.au

0418 136 440

MOUNTAIN BIKE TASMANIA

www.mountainbiketasmania.com.au

0447 712 638

MOTO ADVENTURE TASMANIA

and Hobart Bike Hire

35 Hunter Street Hobart
www.motoadventure.com.au

0499 506 700

LIVE HISTORY

Judith Cornish
judith@livehistoryhobart.com.au

03 6229 8959

PAR AVION

(See Hobart by air)

www.paravion.com.au

03 6248 5390

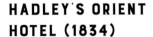

HADLEY'S ORIENT HOTEL (1834)

34 Murray Street
HOBART TAS 7000
www.hadleyshotel.com.au

03 6237 2999

(See advertorial pages)

LENNA (1874)

20 Runnymede Street
BATTERY POINT TAS 7004
www.lenna.com.au

03 6232 3900

(See advertorial pages)

THE OLD WOOLSTORE APARTMENT HOTEL (1900)

1 Macquarie Street
HOBART TAS 7000
www.oldwoolstore.com.au

03 6235 5355

(See advertorial pages)

HENRY JONES ART HOTEL (1804)

25 Hunter Street
HOBART TAS 7000
www.thehenryjones.com

03 6210 7700

MACQUARIE MANOR NANT HOTEL (1875)

172 Macquarie Street
HOBART TAS 7000
www.macmanor.com.au

03 6224 4999

THE LODGE ON ELIZABETH (1829)

249 Elizabeth Street
HOBART TAS 7000
www.thelodge.com.au

03 6231 3830

ISLINGTON HOTEL (1847)

321 Davey Street
HOBART TAS 7000
www.islingtonhotel.com

03 6220 2123

THE ELMS OF HOBART (1917)

452 Elizabeth Street
NORTH HOBART TAS 7000
www.theelmsofhobart.com

03 6231 3277

CRABTREE HOUSE (1840)

130 Crabtree Road
GROVE TAS 7109
www.crabtreehouse.com.au

0429 626 640

GATTONSIDE HERITAGE ACCOMMODATION (1880S)

51-53 Sandy Bay Road
HOBART TAS 7000
www.redawnings.com.au

1800 618 010

RYDGES HOTEL (1842/1889)

393 Argyle Street
NORTH HOBART TAS 7000
www.rydges.com

03 6231 1588

BUNDALL'S BED AND BREAKFAST (1840)

80 New Town Road
NEW TOWN TAS 7008
www.bendallsaccommodation.com

03 6228 2152

LAUREL COTTAGES RICHMOND (1830)

9 Wellington Street
RICHMOND TAS 7025
www.laurelcottages.com.au

03 6260 2397

ORANA HOUSE B&B (1909)

20 Lowelly Road
LINDISFARNE TAS 7015
www.oranahouse.com

03 6243 0404

CUSTOMS HOUSE WATERFRONT HOTEL (1846)

1 Murray Street
HOBART TAS 7000
www.customshouse.com

03 6234 6645

WREST POINT HOTEL CASINO (WREST POINT RIVIERA HOTEL - 1939)

410 Sandy Bay Rd
SANDY BAY TAS 7005
www.wrestpoint.com.au

03 6221 1888

THE OLD BISHOP'S QUARTERS (1837)

26 Fitzroy Place
SANDY BAY TAS 7005
www.bishopsquarters.com.au

0423 182 490

CLEBURNE HOMESTEAD (1820S)

1036 East Derwent Highway
RISDON COVE TAS 7017
www.visitcleburne.com.au

0404 472 793

MEMORY LANE COTTAGES (1890)

130 Brisbane Street
HOBART 7000
www.waverleycottages.com

0408 125 049

CLAREMONT HOUSE (1839)

12 Lady Clark Avenue
CLAREMONT TAS 7011
www.claremonthouse.com.au

03 6249 8818

SEASONS OF TASMANIA (1890S)

14-20 Lewis Street
NORTH HOBART 7000
www.waverleycottages.com

0408 125 049

UNDINE COLONIAL ACCOMMODATION (1816)

6 Dodson Street
ROSETTA 7010
www.undine.net.au

6273 3600

WERNDEE (1903)

1 Mortimer Ave
MOUNT STUART TAS 7000
www.werndee.com.au

03 6228 3844

ASTOR PRIVATE HOTEL (1922)

157 Macquarie Street
HOBART TAS 7000
www.astorprivatehotel.com.au

03 6234 6611

THE QUEEN MARY CLUB (1843)

143 Macquarie Street
HOBART TAS 7000
www.qmchobart.com.au

03 6234 5955

GRANDE VUE HOTEL (1906)

8 Mona Street
BATTERY POINT TAS 7004
www.grandevuehotel.com.au

03 6223 8216

BATTERY POINT BED AND BREAKFAST (1906)

74 Hampden Road
BATTERY POINT TAS 7004

03 6223 3124

BATTERY POINT MANOR (1834)

13-15 Cromwell Street
BATTERY POINT TAS 7004
www.batterypointmanor.com.au

COLVILLE COTTAGE (1877)

32 Mona Street
BATTERY POINT TAS 7004
www.inn.com.au

03 6223 6968

PORTSEA PLACE (1850S)

62 Montpelier Retreat
BATTERY POINT TAS 7004
www.portseaplace.com.au

0409 649 158

MERRE BE'S (1901)

17 Gregory Street
SANDY BAY TAS 7005
www.merrebes.com.au

03 6224 2900

CLYDESDALE MANOR (1880S)

292 Sandy Bay Road
SANDY BAY TAS 7005
www.redawnings.com.au

03 6223 7289

GREGORY HOUSE (VICTORIAN ERA)

24 Gregory Street
SANDY BAY TAS 7005
www.redawnings.com.au

0418 877 026

EDINBURGH GALLERY B&B 1908

211 Macquarie Street
HOBART TAS 7004
www.artac.com.au

03 6224 9229

GRAND OLD DUKE

31 Hampden Road
BATTERY POINT TAS 7004
www.grandolduke.com.au

0400 634 227

TANTALLON LODGE

8 Mona Street
BATTERY POINT TAS 7004

03 6224 1724

YouDo

HOBART HISTORY WALKS

YouDo Hobart History Walks have been operating since 2015, bringing to life the formation of the first settlement through story telling. Warren Glover the author of "Discovering Hobart" is an experienced guide who utilises the oldest buildings in Hobart as the back drop for an evolving story from Hobart's humble and troubled beginning in 1803 - 1804 through the transportation of convicts, early industry, governors, public execution, architecture and much more. Daily walks depart at 1.30pm and 3.30pm and bookings are essential.

HOBART TASMANIA | P: 0439 346 838
www.youdohobart.com

LENNA OF HOBART HOTEL

Lenna of Hobart is not just a place to rest your head. It's an experience. Open the door to this 1874-built sandstone mansion and connect with Hobart Town's story. This landmark hotel puts you right on the historic doorstep of Hobart's vibrant waterfront. Salamanca Place, home to Australia's largest outdoor market and fine eateries are a few hundred metres away and a short walk leads to the CBD, Mona ferry terminal and waterfront precinct.

173

20 RUNNYMEDE STREET HOBART TASMANIA | P: 03 6232 3900
www.lenna.com.au

DAILY TOURS!

CASCADES FEMALE FACTORY HISTORIC SITE

A tribute to the industry of women

The World Heritage listed Cascades Female Factory is Australia's most significant historic site associated with female convicts. It was a purpose built, self-contained institution intended to reform female convicts and is the place to discover the stories of Australia's convict women. Visiting the site today can be both emotional and rewarding, creating a connection with the stories of female convicts in Australia and their children – stories that are often tragic, but that also inspire hope and resilience.

Join a Heritage Tour with an experienced guide who will offer insights into the regimented system of punishment and reform that operated within these walls, and pose the question whether these women were more sinned against than sinning? Part history lesson, part roaming theatre show; experience a performance of Her Story for an accurate and emotional depiction of the harsh life within the Cascades Female Factory in 1833.

16 DEGRAVES ST SOUTH HOBART TASMANIA | P: 1800 139 478
www.femalefactory.org.au

HERBACEOUS TOURS

Explore the fascinating world of Tasmanian food and wine with Herbaceous Tours. Tours include;

- Meet the maker and farm tours
- Make your own sloe gin
- Garden tours
- National parks
- Iconic tourist destinations

Half day, full day or multiple day tours, the choice is yours so let us help you to make wonderful memories of your trip to Tasmania.

HOBART TASMANIA
www.herbaceoustours.com.au

THEATRE ROYAL

VISITING HOBART?

SEE A SHOW, TAKE A TOUR.

29 CAMPBELL STREET HOBART | **03 6233 2299**
www.theatreroyal.com.au

176

HADLEY'S ORIENT HOTEL

Hadley's Orient Hotel, affectionately known as the *Grand old Dame of Hobart*, has nestled in the heart of this vibrant city and in the fond memories of many a guest for over 180 years. Steeped in history, the property has known many names, owners and guises during its existence, becoming an iconic venue in the Hobart landscape.

The heritage-listed Hadley's plays host to almost two centuries of stories, scandals and secrets to be explored. Tread the floor boards as they whisper of the hotel's rich and often tumultuous history. Wander the halls that house memories of gentlemen's lunches, nights of cabaret, and the most marvellous soirées. Wrap yourself in the very fabric of the property - woven with tales of convicts, entrepreneurs, celebrities-past, and countless other patrons of days gone by. Hadley's is committed to providing a unique guest experience, delivering heritage accommodation and signature experiences of unsurpassed quality in Tasmania. Exemplary customer service complements outstanding facilities, extensive guest services and graceful design. The charming venue boasts 71 elegantly styled accommodation suites and is home to a range of guest facilities including the distinguished George Cartwright Room, celebrated Orient Bar, and sun-bathed Atrium – the setting for their renowned traditional Afternoon Tea Experience.

Afternoon Tea has been an institution at Hadley's for many years. Diners enjoy a selection of fine loose leaf teas accompanied by the quintessential three-tiered stand consisting of Hadley's freshly baked signature scones, delicate sandwiches, delightful savouries, and traditional sweet treats reminiscent of the Victorian era. Attentive service complements the finest quality *Noritake* china. From the hand-crafted wooden tea display menu, to the crisp white linen, to the quaint sugar cubes and tongs - no detail is overlooked.

Open daily, Hadley's Gallery presents an exhibition of three artists active in Tasmania during the nineteenthcentury. The exhibition features reproductions of watercolours, drawings and lithographs that highlight the popular themes of the period. A selection of works by John Skinner Prout, Francis Guillemard Anne Meredith reveal the artistic curiosity of colonial artists as they engaged with the Tasmanian landscape.

Located in the heart of the historic CBD amidst an array of boutique shops and chic eateries, Hadley's is just a short stroll from a range of some of Hobart's most popular activities, attractions and cultural experiences. But the property is so much more than just a place to stay whilst exploring the city – Hadley's is an experience in itself.

A traditional afternoon tea experience.

178

34 MURRAY STREET HOBART TASMANIA | P: 03 6237 2999
www.hadleyshotel.com.au

THE OLD WOOLSTORE APARTMENT HOTEL

In days of old the waterfront of Sullivan's Cove was Hobart Town's most notorious area. Today it is a vibrant inner-city location where the welcoming heritage façade of The Old Woolstore masks Tasmania's finest apartment hotel and conference venue. Renowned for spacious rooms and friendly hospitality, the property is centrally located a block from Hobart's waterfront and just a gentle stroll to Salamanca Place with its legendary market, restaurants, bars, galleries and waterside festivities such as the annual Taste Festival. Built behind the veneer of an original wool storage facility constructed in the late 1800s and listed with the National Trust Register, the initial development of The Old Woolstore opened in 1997 with 118 suites. September 2001 saw the completion of an additional 124 apartments, new reception area, gym, Stockmans Restaurant, The Baaa Bar and state-of-the-art event facilities.

During the redevelopment of the site many of the original aspects were retained and feature throughout the hotel today, adding to the character of the property and embracing its often colourful history. The exterior of the Roberts & Co. Woolstore, including its prominent saw-tooth roofline,

was preserved along with the façade of Simpson Soap and Candle Manufactory, on which the words 'J. Kitchen & Son' can still be seen. The restaurant and bar incorporate the old Red Lion Tavern, originally the Bridge Inn Hotel (circa 1850) and an eight foot high historical brick wall built with both convict and 'crest' bricks in the 1870s, now restored." With original grandeur, the heritage listed venue combines old world charm with modern facilities and exceptional service. Accommodation consists of a unique choice of fully serviced apartments and hotel rooms; the decor is contemporary and rooms immaculately presented. All rooms are individually air conditioned and feature Tasmanian Oak and leather furnishings, luxury bedding, free high-speed internet, extra-large screen television with over 35 complimentary channels, Mini-Baaa, luxury Appelles Apothecary bathroom amenities range, plus tea, coffee and toast making facilities. Apartments are fully self-contained offering both laundry and kitchen - perfect for preparing the gourmet produce you will likely collect on your travels through Tasmania.

Rustic charm abounds

180

1 MACQUARIE STREET HOBART TASMANIA | P: 03 6235 5355
www.oldwoolstore.com.au

ABOUT WARREN GLOVER

In 1836 Albert Glover, a seventeen-year-old seaman, is on a four-month voyage from England to Van Diemens Land. The ship he is working on strikes trouble and is broken up upon rocks. Swimming ashore, he finds safety and assistance in a small East Coast town. He stays and marries the local licensee's daughter, Jane Makepeace. This is the story of the first ancestor on my father's side to arrive in Hobart. His son married an immigrant from Germany, who was born on a ship's voyage in 1856 losing a sister she would never know on the same trip. The Glovers stayed in Oatlands for the next 40 years before moving to Bushy Park in the Derwent Valley. That's where my pop was born, and the house is still there.

Margaret McGregor, a Glaswegian, was found with counterfeit money on her person, and was sentenced to seven years transportation to Van Diemens Land. She was 27 years old and married with two children. She was never able to return home and her husband and first child were unable to join her, James, her second child, was allowed to sail with his convict mother as he was not yet weaned, but sadly died on the voyage. Margaret married a convict, William Oakes, a soldier sentenced to seven years for insubordination.

Once they were settled together, living in the slum area of Wapping, they raised two sons and came to be known in the district as a couple of happy drunks. Their happy unity came to an end, though, when Margaret was found by her son, bashed to death in her own bed. Her inconsolable husband was arrested at her bedside. He was found guilty of her murder and sentenced to hang at the Campbell Street Gaol. This was changed to life imprisonment; however, he died of pneumonia nine months later. The Oakes' grandsons would go on to find local fame and become men of legend.

Walter Oakes became the Commissioner of Police, responsible for keeping Hobart clear of crime syndicates from Sydney and Melbourne. His first cousin, my great-grandfather Courtland Oakes, was an incredible athlete, winning sprints, long-distance races and strength tests, all at the same carnival in Queenstown. He would go on to become Tasmanian heavyweight boxing champion for 12 years running, fighting interstate challengers at the Theatre Royal in Hobart. Courtland was employed as a ranger for the Cascade Brewery estate, living in a home above the brewery where he and his wife would raise their 16 children. Courtland knew Mount Wellington like the back of his hand, tending to its fire trails, walking tracks and numerous huts and rescuing lost walkers, including a young Errol Flynn, who was missing for a night and two days. When found, he was given a sound kick in the pants. Courtland was a brewery employee for 60 years and died at age 92 on a Cascade pension.

ABOUT PAUL COUNTY

Paul Brendan County is a fifth generation Tasmanian photographer, cook, teacher and publisher. He worked for many years in the hospitality industry and also completed a Bachelor of Fine Arts degree majoring in photography and a Bachelor of Teaching degree. His love of storytelling and fascination with Tasmania's hospitality community led him to found The Culinary Historians of Tasmania in 1998.

His father, Peter, a real Hobart lad, grew up playing on Hobart's streets. His family home at 9 Melville Street, was between the Hobart Penitentiary Gaol and the Fire Brigade. His uncle, Bill County, a carpenter who built sets at the Theatre Royal down the road, frequented the Ocean Child Hotel, established in 1844, only a stone's throw away from the family home.

The County family has a long history in Hobart public service. Paul's grandfather Rupert James County worked for the Postmaster General's Department (now Australia Post) and for many years at the Hobart GPO, as did his uncle Harold, a telecommunications technician.

Paul's great-grandfather Thomas County was an Irish sailor in the English navy and emigrated to Tasmania in the mid 1800s. He worked in the Treasury department and was requested by Premier Philip Fysh to be the custodian of the Customs House on his retirement. Paul's parents, Peter and Patricia, also worked in the public service and his uncle Thomas County commenced work at the transport commission at 14 and retired as the head of motor registry. Paul has one son, Henry, a keen family researcher and historian.

ABOUT CATHY MCAULIFFE

Cathy McAuliffe has been working as an art director, graphic designer and illustrator for over 15 years. She specialises in creating graphics and illustrations for young people, maps for publications and corporate identities. She also loves creating unique book designs, historical public artworks and hand lettering, using a mix of traditional and modern techniques.

Her mother's first job was working at the Cadbury's Chocolate factory in the recruitment department. Her father began his working life at Hobart's EZ company as a metalurgist, later pursuing his interest in zinc and lead production.